Eggemoggin Reach Review

Volume II

An Anthology of Prose and Poetry by Members of
The Deer Isle Writers' Group

&

The Eggemoggin Writers' Collaborative

MANAGING EDITOR
Maureen Farr

MANUSCRIPT COORDINATOR
Norma Sheard

TREASURER
Leslie Dyanne

BUSINESS MANAGER
Anne L. Burton
email: Reachreview2@verizon.net

COVER IMAGE
"Strange Writings"
Egg tempera on panel by
Phil Schirmer
Inspired by the poem, "Stone," by Charles Simic

PUBLISHED BY
Eggemoggin Reach Review
PO Box 376, Deer Isle, Maine 04627

Book Design by Mozelle! Studio
maureenfarr@verizon.net

PRINTED IN USA

Eggemoggin Reach Review ISBN   978-0-9755586-1-4

Eggemoggin Reach Review Volume II is available by mail for $21.50, including postage and 5% Maine State sales tax. Please send $21.50 via US mail: Eggemoggin Reach Review, 32 Burnt Cove Road, Stonington, ME 04681.

CONTENTS

CONTENTS

CONTENTS

Acknowledgments

This volume is dedicated to the memory of Billie Hotaling, a former member of the Deer Isle Writers' Group, who once remarked on an author's characterization of writer's block, "Oh, for heaven's sake, he should just pull up his socks and write!"

To each and every writer who submitted work for this volume, and to all those who supported us in more ways than we can count, thank you.

Three years ago, a group of 28 writers got together and worked hard to produce Volume I of *Eggemoggin Reach Review*. That process took almost exactly nine months from our first meeting to the day we held the finished book in our hands. We were all as excited as any parents of a newborn.

Before Volume I was even printed, we each made a list of friends and family who were potential buyers; letters were sent asking for pre-orders, and we raised enough money to pay for printing. After the book came out, readings and signings were scheduled, coordinated, and managed; a host of volunteers took books to stores and galleries to sell — and the book was a big success.

Soon, people were asking when Volume II would appear, and we realized it was time to get back to work — and back to work we went. We wrote poems, short stories, bits and pieces of memoir, truth, and fiction. We attended writers' group meetings, critiquing and guiding one another through the sometimes long process of writing, editing, and rewriting. The end results can be found in these pages.

Eggemoggin Reach connects Penobscot Bay and Jericho Bay, and flows between Deer Isle and the Blue Hill Peninsula. We chose the name *Eggemoggin Reach Review* because our contributing authors live and write on both sides of this beautiful body of water.

Eggemoggin Reach Review

Volume II

Judi K. Beach

"God's Eldest Daughter"
—Thomas Fuller, D.D.

In the dark beginning, out of love
for creation, he birthed her.
"Let there be light" and in the deep
immensity, a glory of luminescence,
a phosphorescent radiance appeared.

Light, the first narcissus, wanting
to dazzle and sparkle, to blaze and
twinkle, had been wandering all day
(though it was eons) without a place
to rest. So her father said, "Firmament,"
and she was appeased for a while
seeing her luster mirrored in the stars,
but an eternity spent looking at her
unchanging self grew dull.

She demanded a brighter future
and her heavenly father took pity,
said, "Water," and Light delighted
in the order of her rainbow, in the way
she could float like loose threads
on the waves, make a path over the ocean
under pricks of starlight, zigzag
in puddles. She saw herself fractured
and sutured and was amused for a while,
but soon became bored.

So her father said, "Let there be life,"
and Light grew enamored of green
and the fireworks of blossoms, the way
she could be small, be tall, shape herself
into fruit, twine as vines, cling like lichen.
She fell in love with the rough-smooth,
soft-hard of life, the jagged-ripple-slick
of life, the crinkle and wrinkle of it,
the furrows and foliage. Light warmed
herself in fur, took flight in feathers, ran
across meadows in candescent celebration,
but still, after a while, burned for more.

Once more her ever-patient father
went to the beach and gathered crystals
of sand and pressed them into his image.
Light beamed with the many ways
mortals would know her, the auras
cast round them, the paths
to their enlightenment. Light
learned to wink and blink. She
glared and flared and flashed
with brilliance. She haloed the holy
and let her pride shine. She glistened
with sweat and sparked imagination.
But of all the gifts Light bestowed
on humans, her favorite was to stand
at the end of a dark tunnel
and offer a glimmer of hope.

Judi K. Beach

Lido 1924
after a painting by Max Beckman

We all go to the beach expecting sunshine
and a little fun. We lie down on clean towels
and shake sand from our shoes. But here
by the sea, fresh air wrapped around us,
we settle in for the long undertaking.

Some go into the water blindly. Some go
clutching a prayer. Some seem to enjoy it,
and some look to us to save them.
But soon enough we will be swimming
with them. The lights of the city
we have lived in will be pale yellow petals
floating on the waves. Even those
who can't swim are washed
into the water by the insistence of tide.

There are picnic baskets big as caskets
and whole clans eat from them.
When a wave plucks one, a favorite
grandparent, perhaps, the rest slowly follow
as though an anchor had been dropped
and link by link the entire family
is dragged into the water.

Two children build a sandcastle,
thc only permanence they'll know.
Each mother eyes her child.
Most husbands swim first as if testing
the waters. They call back to us,
"Not too cold." They have tasted
the wet wisdom and think they know
the sweet-bitter-salt of it for us all.

A wife wearing a cloche wraps herself
in a robe so she won't burn
and walks to the edge of the water.
A sister tries to stand firm as the undertow
pulls her in. A father's head is barely
visible, and the son thinks it's all play
while the daughter walks the sand
between tide marks, looks back at us
as if to say, "You could be next."

Judi K. Beach

Rounds

My sister washes while I dry and put away.
How long it takes, doing dishes, when she'd
rather be reading, and I'd rather be outside
climbing the buckeye that shades our childhood
until the sky, studded with stars, is a billboard
telling me when to come down, when to go home.

At the sink, sometimes she, sometimes I
begin singing, *Bluebonnets, bluebonnets*
with your coats so blue... and the other joins
in harmony, the edge of our enthusiasm
splitting the verse into rounds, our teamed voices
rising like steam from the dishwater.

We are immersed in song, forgetting
any arguments we'd had that afternoon
over who would vacuum and who would dust.
Our voices find their places side by side
as glasses and forks, cups and plates, slide
from my sister's wet hands into my towel,

our voices delighting in what they do
together, how they ring around the kitchen
filling every space, every cabinet and cupboard,
even the pantry with the dark secret of why
we were never encouraged to find with each other
what harmony we could.

Later we would lose even that closeness,
moving to separate coasts as if to get as far away
from each other as possible, though that wasn't true.
It was Ohio we were fleeing and parts of our lives:
our parents' angers that swelled and crashed
like derelict tides, our fears of drowning.

Now we come together as women, the table
of our parents no longer between us. In her kitchen
my sister minces garlic. I brush around her
and draw warm water into the sink and begin,
with cloth and a round of *Bluebonnets*, the slow
circular motion of finding our togetherness again.

Double Agent

Chapter One

"Do you think Mathew knows? I'd be surprised if he didn't. He's not dumb. Be careful, you're dripping on your patio."

"Well, push me over some newspaper to drip on. Of course he doesn't know. It just wouldn't occur to him to wonder. Damn, I made a mess of that one. Hand me a tissue."

"Faith, come on, I'm your sister not your servant."

"Same thing." Faith smiled and finished painting her last toenail. "I'm sure he doesn't know, but even if he did I wouldn't give a damn. You know how remote and private he is, especially lately."

Admiring her sister's feet, Charity kicked off her sandals and began removing her old polish.

"Pass me the tissues and shove over the newspaper. How did you hold your foot up so high? I can't breathe."

Faith laughed. "Stop eating."

Soon both women sat back, letting their toes dry while they watched Faith's two and Charity's three children insult and chase each other in and out of the pool. Faith told them to go into the kitchen and make themselves something to eat. Within an hour Charity left for home, her kids bickering and arguing in the back seat.

"Call me later."

"I will," said Faith as she entered the house. She sighed at the mess in the kitchen but decided not to call her children to help clean it. She didn't think she could stand the noise and energy that would entail. As she cleaned, she thought about her job, which was neither very good nor very bad, but seemed like heaven now because of Luke. Hard to believe it'd only been seven weeks on Friday. She wondered if he'd remember. Most men aren't very good about that sort of thing. Mathew never remembered any date except Christmas.

She wiped off the counter tops, closed the dishwasher, made a cup of tea, and let her mind go back over every detail of the last time she and Luke had been together. They drove separately to The Full Moon Motel, which was quite far out of town. Faith arrived, according to their usual arrangement, a little after he did. He was standing in the middle of the room dressed for the office in a suit, white shirt and tie. They did not embrace, but exchanged gleeful grins.

He said, "Would you please remove your clothing, ma'am?"

"Sure, but you better loosen your tie."

She started slowly, holding the first piece of clothing in her finger tips until Luke started singing *A Pretty Girl Is Like A Melody*. He had a clear, true tenor voice, and she stripped and danced while he sang holding an imaginary microphone. She stopped as she removed the final article, her panties. She had taken a rather nasty fall the time before while trying to dance and step out of them at the same time. Luke pulled back the bedding and stacked the pillows against the headboard.

"Your seat, madam." He moved to the center of the room and started singing *Lady Be Good* as he danced and disrobed.

Faith loved to watch him dance. He was good and the more clothing he removed, the more abandoned he became. As soon as he was naked, he turned his back to her, took the belt out of his trousers and fastened it around his waist. Then he tucked his tie over the belt, letting it hang down over his penis. He turned, posed, then started to sing,

"I'd love to get you on a slow boat to China, all to myself alone," while he danced slowly and sensually closer and closer to the bed. This was a new act, and Faith hooted, whistled, clapped and said, "Your cravat has too much starch in it."

With a pounce he was in bed, running his hands slowly over her body, complimenting every part he touched. Being thirty something and the mother of two, she could have listened all day, but smiled as he entered her and responded without words or thoughts until they lay tangled together telling each other how great it was. They dozed, still entwined.

Luke finally sat up and said he had a meeting at his church to go to. Sometimes they showered together, but Faith burrowed into the pillows and drowsed until he was ready to leave, then stood up, put her arms around him, pressing her warm naked body against his suit. He gave her a quick, hard kiss and left.

Faith knew Luke was a religious man, as was her husband. This had alarmed her at first. What was it about her that drew these Bible thumpers? With Luke it seemed to add an extra dimension, erotic and mysterious. Why it turned her on, she didn't know or care. Of course, when he insisted he could cure what ailed her, headache, backache, or whatever, by laying on hands, she knew damn well why. Other than that, she didn't think about it much. Just enjoy, she told herself.

Little mini vacations from reality; exactly what I need, she thought, her head in the freezer as she pawed through the shelves for the package of chicken parts she remembered seeing a while ago. She set them out to defrost, went to change her clothes and stopped to tell the children, Hope, eleven, and Brian, nine, to hang out their suits and towels.

Later, supper was over, kids were in bed, Mathew was still at a church meeting where he had gone right after the morning service. She picked out clothes for work in the morning, glad the weekend was over and she would see Luke.

She got in bed and called Charity who was definitely a little jealous of Faith's affair. The sisters had always wanted what the other one had. Charity retaliated by harping on the dangers involved in 'seeing someone.'

"Are you in bed yet?" Charity said.

"Of course, aren't you?"

"Yeah, can't you hear the snores coming out of your brother-in-law?"

"Lord, what a racket. How do you stand it?"

"Oh, I'm used to it; kind of soothing. Are you alone?" she whispered.

"Mmm hmm, Mathew's still at his church meeting."

"That's not exactly what I meant," said Charity.

Faith hiked herself further up on her pillows and waited almost a minute, smiling at the phone in her hand, not speaking.

"Faith, you mean he's right there now?" Her voice hissed as she spoke.

"What do you think?" she said. "See you tomorrow."

"Faith!"

"Bye." She hung up.

She had never discussed the intimate details of her affair with Charity or anyone else. She wondered why; they usually discussed everything. Probably to keep it more special and apart from the rest of her life. She liked it that way, and didn't tell Luke anything about her husband and kids.

Mathew came home later than usual from his church gathering. She thought about getting up and fixing him a plate of food, then heard the microwave. She got up anyway and got a glass of fizzy water. Mathew was sitting at the kitchen table.

"Hi, you ran late."

"Yeah, there were people from two or three different churches. It took longer."

He was reading the paper while he ate and didn't look up.

"Get enough to eat?"

"Mmm hmm."

"There's ice cream and brownies. The kids made them."

"OK."

Faith drank half a glass of water and stood for a moment looking at him. "Goodnight."

He glanced at her. "'night."

Back in bed, eyes open in the dark, she wondered if he was seeing anyone. She had never thought so, but it could be. Who would want him? I guess he's not bad looking really, she admitted. He's not very exciting, but maybe some women would think so.

Faith arrived at work a little early the next day and sat at her desk. She was still perplexed about her husband's total lack of interest in her. He had never

15

been exactly affectionate, but they had been closer than they were now. They even used to have sex.

They had met at a party fifteen years earlier. He was handsome and quiet. Probably deep, she'd thought, which in her mind back then was just a small step away from being sexy. He'd looked in her eyes with an intense expression and talked for a long time about extruding aluminum.

She pretended to listen while wondering how it would be to make out with him. He drove her home and told her, on the way, how many loads of gravel had been used to repair the stretch of road they were traveling. She was amused and decided he was just very shy and awkward talking to girls.

Outside her parents' house he said, "Maybe I'll see you again sometime." He still hadn't smiled.

Faith smiled and said, "I hope so." Then she leaned toward him and kissed his cheek.

He was very still for a few seconds, then grabbed her to him, kissed her passionately, stopped, put his hands on the steering wheel and said, "I'll call you." He looked straight ahead. She opened her door, climbed out and went in the house, bemused and confused.

Faith shook her head at the memories, turned on her computer and started on the stack of work in front of her just as Luke stopped by her desk and handed her some papers, saying, "See what you can do with these, please." He winked quickly and walked away.

The next morning, as Luke's note suggested, she called in sick, got the kids off to school and Mathew off to work. She tried to remember when she and Mathew had stopped kissing each other hello and goodbye. Whatever, she thought, but knew she missed it a little. She showered, dressed carefully and drove to the same motel as last time.

Luke was affectionate and sensual, made her feel sexy and beautiful, but he seemed a little distracted. They pretty much got in bed and made love; no singing, no dancing. They lay together a little while after, but he soon said he had to get going. Faith was annoyed and made sure she gathered up her clothes, got in the bathroom first and closed the door. She could act remote and distracted too, damn it. She left as soon as she was dressed, called a breezy "Bye" to the bathroom door, and went out to her car.

Nevertheless, she mused as she headed home, even less than perfect sex was a great way to start the morning. Languid, that's what I feel. She thought about going into work in the afternoon, but knew she wouldn't get docked for taking the whole day off.

Faith loved being in the house alone. It had a very different feel, calm, orderly in spite of the clutter. She settled down to read a novel. Sunshine streamed in, and of course, she drifted off and awoke an hour later. The lazy, self indulgent mood had vanished, and she started to think about Luke. She knew he was married and had some kids. Other than that, she knew nothing. She had never before even wondered. It's better not knowing. This was an affair for short episodes of escape only.

The children came home hungry, full of news, requests and complaints.

"What's to eat?"

"I need lunch money for tomorrow."

"A guy in my class broke his foot. He's got a cool cast."

"Casts aren't cool. They're hot and itchy, dummy."

"Shut up. You don't know everything. Mom, make her mind her own business."

"Can it," said Faith, setting out a box of graham crackers and a jar of peanut butter. Eventually they pulled homework out of their backpacks and quiet, if not peace, prevailed. Besides, she thought, returning to her musings about Luke while she made meat balls, it's strictly the sex for both of us, friendly, fun, affectionate sex. There was one thing that seemed strange, though, remembering the morning's tryst. While she was in the bathroom afterwards with the door ajar to let out the steam, she had caught a glimpse of him reflected in the bathroom mirror. He was on his knees next to the bed praying, eyes closed, face raised toward the ceiling, hands clasped like a picture in a Sunday School book. Was he giving thanks or asking for forgiveness? She didn't feel comfortable about trying to get an explanation. She didn't particularly like to hear people's thoughts about God.

Faith did go to church most Sundays with Mathew and the children because she thought she should. It had always been an important part of Mathew's life. He never really discussed his religious feelings with her, except that he didn't believe in sex before marriage. She wished that hadn't been the case. She might not have married him if she could have tried him out first. She really hadn't been all that experienced herself, only that hunk of a hockey player, and, well, his older brother just that once. So who knows?

Mathew's widowed mother, whom Faith wanted to like but didn't, had a sad, fatalistic attitude. She related everything, from the death of a neighbor to an overcooked roast, to God by way of the Bible. Poor Mathew. He was an only child and still strongly attached to her.

"She's a very worthy woman," he said often.

During the past year Mathew had become a deacon, serving on committees and recruiting new members. Thankfully he had stopped trying to get her involved. She was glad to have him out several nights a week. He was becoming increasingly dreary. She was usually asleep when he came home, but would wake up bleary eyed and squint at the clock.

Autumn moved ahead. Shrubs were draped in huge wispy webs; inflatable pumpkins and plastic witches lounged on porches next to small sheaves of straw. On a Saturday in October, Faith, Charity and the kids were going to a soccer game in which some of their children were playing.

"Come on, Mathew, come with us," said Faith. "You haven't been to a game yet this year."

He looked at his feet, then the sky and cleared his throat. "Sorry, I've got a lot of church work to catch up on. Umm, some phone calls and things."

"You used to enjoy the games. We'll only be an hour or so. Oh, all right, do your church stuff."

She had been irritable lately, but tried not to let it show. Luke and she had met only once in the last several weeks, and he had cancelled one other time. He acted differently with her now, obviously avoiding any chance to have even a friendly chat. She knew it was bound to end, but would have liked to make it a mutual decision and not just be discarded like a piece of junk mail.

Maybe I'll just pray about it, she thought. I'll ask God to give him mumps. She got in her car and slammed the door.

"Faith,"whispered Charity. "Are you OK? Are you still you know what?"

"If you whisper, they just pay more attention."

"What are you guys talking about?" demanded Hope from the back seat.

"Halloween."

"Boring," called back a different voice.

They drove the rest of the way without talking. After they parked, the children swarmed out and disappeared. Faith and Charity climbed up the bleachers and sat.

"These seats are hard," said Charity.

"Your tush is pretty well cushioned; stop bitching."

"I notice you can sit very comfortably for a long time, so don't talk to me about padding."

"I'm just a tough, lean mean machine."

"Faith, what's wrong?" Charity opened a bag of pretzels and offered them to her.

"Oh, nothing I didn't expect. It's over. But we didn't even talk about it or anything. I'm just pissed."

Charity crunched pretzels and then said, "I'm sorry."

"Thanks. I'll be OK."

"Have you and Mathew been getting along? Things seem kind of strained."

Faith unwrapped a stick of gum and started chewing. "No, I guess we aren't. I know he isn't aware of Luke. I'd know if he was. He's just… Yay, way to go! One to nothing! They look pretty good. He's just totally withdrawn from all of us. His mind is somewhere else; at church, I guess."

"Have you tried to talk to him about it?"

"Yeah. He just clams up and looks, well, kind of nervous and sad."

They sat and watched the game. Their team won, and the the kids were wild on the way home. Faith pulled into McDonald's. "Treat's on me, but behave yourselves or you'll wait in the car." The feeding frenzy was over in half an hour, and they returned to their own houses. Mathew's car was still in the driveway.

Faith went into his study. He was on the phone and hung up as she came in.

"Great game. You should've come. Our brilliant son made a goal."

"Great. I'll try to get to the next one. I got a lot done today while it was quiet here. Faith...." He looked at her and took off his glasses. He always looked terribly vulnerable to her without them.

"Matt, is something bothering you?"

"Why?"

"You seem sad and kind of far away."

He looked down at his desk, evened up some papers, put them in a pile. "I guess I do."

Faith sat down in the extra chair and tucked her hair behind her ear. "You do what?"

"What you said. About feeling sad and far away. Life just gets..." he paused, straightened out a paper clip. "Life isn't simple. Some things are so complicated." He shrugged. "My mind gets crazy when I try to sort everything out."

"I always thought you knew, better than most of us, what you were doing. You always seem so sure."

"I know. I always thought I did too. I thought I always did do right, but maybe not. I just don't know."

He looked out the window at the backyard where a group of crows strutted and parried with each other as they searched for stray bird seed. "Being a crow looks easier than being a man."

"Come on, Matt, you know you don't like to poop outside."

He smiled. "You're always pretty good about accepting me the way I am. It's probably not easy. Sometimes I can't even accept myself."

"I guess I've always thought you live on a little bit higher moral plane than I do. Of course I never try to pull myself up there with you."

She reached out to touch his clenched hands planted on the desk, but stopped and said, "You're right, life is hard, but it's OK to have fun sometimes."

He looked at her. "Fun is almost as hard as real life."

Faith said, "Fun is the part of life that makes it easier."

He shook his head slightly, "No."

"Mathew, do you love me?"

"Yes. I love you and I love the children."

"It's hard to tell sometimes, like recently, and I guess I've had some doubts myself."

They sat in silence.

Faith sat up straight. "Let's go for a walk. The kids'll be OK. They're watching a movie. We can go downtown and bring back pizza. It'll be easier to talk, maybe, if we're doing something. This seems a little like being called into the principal's office."

Mathew got up and stepped to the window. His hands were on the side casements, his head pressed against the glass. He turned, and Faith saw a glint of tears.

"I guess we'd better. Do I need a jacket?"

"Just a windbreaker. Unless you don't plan to break any wind."

Faith always started making stupid jokes when she got nervous. She wished she wouldn't.

They asked the kids what they wanted on their pizza.

"Pepperoni."

"Mushrooms."

She and Mathew used to walk so easily together. The pace seemed strained now and awkward.

"We don't have to talk if you don't want to. We could just relax and talk later." She listened to their footsteps and the rustle as they scuffed through fallen leaves. She knew she was being cowardly.

"I think we better start now. It'll take some time, and it's easier without being in the house with the kids."

"OK, you're probably right."

"It's difficult to get started. Well, about a month ago at one of the meetings some people from other churches came."

"I remember, you told me that's why you were so late."

"Yeah, well, there was someone there from the West Side Church who caught my attention. You know, he really made sense and spoke clearly about the issue. He noticed me, too, when I spoke, and we nodded in agreement with each other."

"What was the issue?"

"That's not important now. Let me finish. By the end of the meeting he and I obviously saw the problem the same way. Most of the people there disagreed with us, and it felt so good to have an ally. You know, I've never had many friends." He zipped up his jacket and jammed his hands in the pockets.

"I know," said Faith. "I wonder why."

"I guess it never seemed as important as other things."

"Besides, it might be fun," said Faith. She sounded bitter and realized that's the way she felt.

"When the meeting closed and people filed out, I went into the sanctuary to pray. It was pretty dark in there. I thought I was alone, but I wasn't."

"Who was there?"

"It was the guy I was telling you about. I could see after a few minutes. We were both praying."

"So, did you go out for coffee or something?"

"Here's the pizza place. I'll try to finish telling you on the way home."

It smelled wonderful in the small restaurant. They sat at the counter and had a coke while they waited. Neither one of them could think of anything to say, other than "It sure smells good" and "Did you remember the pepperoni and mushrooms?" They started home, each carrying one pizza, trying to keep the boxes as flat as possible.

"Well," said Faith, "after you prayed, did you spend some time talking?"

"We went out and had a couple of beers."

"You never drink beer."

"I know, but we did."

She listened as they crunched along and caught a faint whiff of woodsmoke as they headed home. "So what's the big deal? You had a few beers."

"We get together now after all my meetings."

"Does he attend them all?"

"Unh unh, hardly any."

"You must have a lot to talk about. I know you don't like to stay out late." She turned her head toward him. "I don't mind. I'm glad you have a friend."

He stopped walking and looked down. He cleared his throat. He looked at her, then away.

"We have a few beers, then go to his apartment."

"Is he married?"

"Um yeah, but…"

Faith laughed, "But his wife would rather have him bring his friends home than stay out drinking. Why don't you bring him to our house sometime? I'd like to meet him."

"He's going through a divorce. He lives alone."

"So? He's probably lonely."

"No. It's different than that."

"Well, I'd still like to meet him even if he's not lonely. Does he have kids?"

"Yeah, I think."

"Maybe he could bring his kids over after church sometime for dinner."

"I don't think that would work out."

"Why? Doesn't he see them?"

"I don't know. We never talk about it."

"Men are so different. It's weird. Women almost always talk about their kids. Don't you think it's odd not to? Have you told him about your family?"

"Some."

"Matt, you're being very evasive. You brought all this up for some reason. Spit it out. You're driving me nuts."

"Maybe it's not a good time to talk."

"Look, we're out of the house, away from the kids. This was your idea. What's wrong?"

"Everything."

"Well, we're almost home, so you better get started."

Mathew shifted the pizza slightly and stared up at the darkening sky. Anguish showed on his face, and the tears flowed.

"Faith, we're lovers."

She felt her pizza start to tip and righted it quickly. She hoped all the toppings hadn't slid to one side.

"Whaddya mean?"

"Faith, for God's sake, we have sex together. We're lovers."

She sat down on the curb, setting the pizza box carefully beside her. Her feet were in the gutter. She wrapped her arms around her drawn up legs, face pressed onto her knees, rocking back and forth slightly. Mathew sat down beside her, his pizza box next to him. He put his arm around her shoulders.

"What'd you say? You're all muffled."

"Who is he?" she repeated..

"What does that matter?"

"It matters. If I had an affair, wouldn't you want to know who with?"

He took his arm off her shoulders. "I never thought about that. No, I wouldn't."

"Well, you've made this my problem now, and I need a name to make it real to me."

Mathew was silent, eyes closed hard. "I have to discuss it with him first."

"God damn it, Mathew, tell me the guy's name."

His face went down between his knees, hands covering the back of his head as if warding off blows. His voice was choked, but Faith heard him clearly.

"Works where you do. Name's Luke." ■

Trapped

"We'll haul two more strings, Viola, and call it a day. You got enough pockets ready?"

"Yeah. Daddy, can I have tomorrow off? Gilbert needs to drive to Rockland to pick up his clutch, and he wants me to go with him."

"No. We need to haul through by tomorrow night. There's a northeaster coming. Might have to miss two, three days. Ask him to wait for bad weather to go."

"He needs it soon as possible so he can put everything back together and get going again. You know that."

"Sorry. With BJ off to college, you're the only helper I got. You told me you'd take brother's place and stick with it if I paid you the same. A deal's a deal. Careful of that snapper there. He's frisky. Jesus, did you measure that one before you tossed him? What's the matter? You sulking? You're a pretty big girl to act like that."

"I'm just fine. I don't want to talk about it. You always, always, always tell me what to do. I'm not a little kid. You never talked that way to BJ, just because he's a guy."

"Just because he don't sass me all the time. I'm your father and the captain of this boat. You work for me. Now shut up and start banding."

"Damn it, after this season that's it for me. You never cared about me anyway. Never, just BJ and your damn boat."

Turning his back to her, he put the boat in gear as he hauled another pair of traps onto the port side deck. A huge swell struck broadside, forcing the boat to pitch violently.

The traps started to slip back into the water. The rope, coiled on the floor, ran out over the stern. He stepped and lunged after the second trap. He missed. The rope whipped around his legs pulling him off balance. With terrible speed he was yanked on to the stern deck. He grabbed for the combing, managed to hold on. He clung there, forearms and torso on the deck. Cold wet legs stretched out and down by the force of the trailing traps. He looked for Viola. He could not see her.

"No!"

He was sure she had gone overboard, down all those fathoms. He saw her at last lying near the bait box.

"Viola, get up, dear, I need you!"

She didn't stir. He called until his voice was hoarse. She never moved.

The force of the traps pulling on his legs was unbearable until he realized that if he shifted his weight more to one arm, the boat began to turn, the tangled traps acting as a kind of rudder.

He knew where they were; not far from a small, rocky island, little more than a ledge. He began to guide the boat by agonizing shifts, praying that Viola was still alive. If he could ram the island the boat would beach itself. He would be able to stand, reach the knife in his belt, cut himself free. He would radio for help, and surely he could save Viola. He shifted again. There was a cracking, splintering noise. The boat shuddered, listed, and the engine went dead. With his numb right arm he fumbled for his knife, not breathing for fear of dropping it. He could barely feel his fingers as he let go of the of the boat. He sank down to the rocks in water up to his chest. Slowly he drew in air, held it, squatted down, and sawed through the rope. He couldn't move his legs for a few moments, but was finally able to wade slowly to the pebbled shore. He lay there one or two minutes while a little strength came back. He managed to kneel, then stand, holding on to the downed side of the boat. Viola was still wedged between a bait box and a partition. With effort he hoisted himself in, took off his gloves, felt her neck for a pulse. It didn't feel very strong. He sat down next to her after radioing for help. He reached over and brushed some hair away from her face and saw blood matted in it. He held her hand. It was cold, so he took both in his and tried to warm them. While he listened for the sound of approaching boats, he told her what had happened.

"I thought you'd been knocked overboard, and I almost just let go. When I saw you, I knew I had to make it."

She remained immobile, eyes closed.

He put a dry jacket over her, took up her hands again then heard the sound of diesel engines. He started to let go, but thought he felt a slight pressure. He tightened his grip and waited. ■

Anne Larkosh Burton

Clothes My Father Wore

What goes on in this house stays in this house.

Daddy roared this commandment thoughout the four-room tenement at 32 Middle Street, whenever he suspected one of us of talking to outsiders about something he considered "family business." Standing close to six feet, with broad shoulders, large hands, hazel eyes flashing in his ruddy, handsome face, he was a commanding presence to me as a pale-blond, pigtailed, eight-year old. His word was law. It grounded my world even more that the commandments I learned from the nuns at Sacred Heart School.

Family secrecy was one of the ways he tried to hide the inadequacy he felt about the poverty of his childhood and his seventh grade education. The clothes he wore was the other way he attempted to cover both shame about his past and mysteries about his present that have puzzled me all my life. To talk about them, even to this day, raises feelings of betrayal and anxiety within my soul.

Most of the people I knew had just two sets of clothes, one for work or play and one for dress. For children, the play clothes were usually hand-me-downs or last year's school dresses or pants, if they were too worn for the next child in line to wear. The adults I knew were factory workers. The women wore old, frayed dresses. The men dressed in denim bib overalls over tattered shirts. I would see them going to and from work, clothing, faces, hands and hair, dirty and grease-stained.

But my Daddy was different. He left the house and returned at night dressed in his second best pants and a freshly ironed shirt. His hair was neatly combed and his hands and face were scrubbed clean. Early each morning my mother prepared two pint bottles sealed with wax paper lined caps and filled with hot coffee. She wrapped them in several layers of newspaper as makeshift thermos bottles. Then Daddy rolled them in clean overalls and carried them to the Nicholson File Company where he worked as a file-cutter. At the end of the day he changed back into his pants and white shirt and came home with the empty bottles rolled in the soiled overalls. He left the overalls in the back hall for Mama to launder on Saturday. He set the empty coffee bottles in the pantry sink for me to wash with the supper dishes.

At home he wore old trousers and a clean white T-shirt. One of my most persistent memories is seeing his broad, T-shirt clad back as he sat at the kitchen table, leaning on the newspaper, arms bound by the tight, short sleeves. Sometimes there were tears under the arm, worn there from the constant movement at his job, but the shirts were always immaculate.

All day long he stood in front of a file-cutting machine, which fed bars of steel from the side into an opening in front of him. As he watched, a sharp-edged cutter descended from within the back of the machine, moving along making ridges in the steel, from the rear end of the bar to within an inch of the pointed end at the front. His job was to insure there were no misses in the pattern of cuts. If he saw that the blade of the cutter had not functioned properly, he had to reach into the machine and quickly remove the imperfect bar and toss it to the side.

Occasionally the machine malfunctioned and failed to stop before it reached the end of the bar. The cutter would continue, hitting the pointed end, flipping it up and hurling it at the operator who must move or risk losing an eye or worse. Daddy must have learned early and well because he was never hurt on the job. His only battle scars were numerous splinters of black steel in the skin of his hands. The filings were impossible to remove, but once in a while, one would become infected and he would lance it out with a needle and a pair of tweezers. But for the most part they remained there until the skin sloughed off. Long after he stopped working in the file company, my father had the filings under his skin.

On Saturday mornings, he would fill a large, oval copper boiler with water, place it on the top of the stove and when it was hot, pour it into the tub of the Easy Spin-Dry washer. Mama would add *Rinso* from the large green and white box and the smell of *Clorox* would fill the house as she washed the white clothes, sheets and underwear and tablecloths. She'd load the wet wash into the "spinning-tub" with its many holes through which the soapy water was removed and fed through a hose hooked over the edge of the pantry sink. More hot water was added to the washtub as she washed the colored dresses and shirts and when these were done, Daddy's dirty overalls.

Then the tub was completely emptied and clean hot water was added from the copper kettle. After each batch was rinsed and spun dry, it was placed in a wide wicker basket that Daddy carried down the stairs to the back yard. I helped Mama hang them on the clotheslines. One line was devoted to his overalls, the heavy load propped up by a wooden clothes pole set at an angle to keep them from dragging on the ground. All this was usually accomplished by ten in the morning and then there was cleaning and shopping to do and in the evening, the ironing.

Later in the afternoon, we children were told to play outside or to stay in the living room. Daddy would set a round galvanized tub in the pantry and fill it with yet another copper boiler full of hot water.

"I wonder who's kissing her now…" We could hear him singing as he scrubbed away the grime and sweat of the past week. When finished with his bath, he poured more hot water into the basin in the sink and worked up a lather in his soap mug with his beaver-bristle shaving brush. He shaved carefully with a single edge razor smoothing an occasional nick with a styptic pencil. The skin on his face glowed shiny and red when he applied the splash of Aqua Velva After-Shave.

"Sometimes I wonder how you spend the lonely night…" He put on his clean white tee shirt and Jockey shorts, black socks, stiffly starched and ironed white shirt and a dark suit. He combed his shiny, *Brillianteen*-ed hair into a pompadour. He gave the toes of his wing-tipped shoes a final buff, knotted his blue and white polka-dotted tie into a perfect bow and stepped into the parlor. How handsome he looked.

"Come kiss your father good-bye," he'd say, leaning down for each of his children to kiss his smooth cheek. "Be good and listen to your mother," would be his parting words.

Where was my mother?

On one occasion I was out in the back yard playing with my sister when Daddy made his Saturday afternoon departure. Danny, a mentally handicapped young boy, (*retarded* we said then) who lived next door called out, "Where ya goin'? Where ya goin'?"

Daddy turned and shouted in anger, "I don't even tell my own kids where I am going, why the hell should I tell you?" Danny ran crying into the house and we stood stock still as Daddy swung around the corner of the house and headed for the front gate. ■

The Shoelace Pairer's Daughter

Some women are tied to their mothers by a talent for singing or sewing, some by the color of their hair or eyes but I am tied to my mother by shoelaces, those neat little bundles of brown, black and white that were wrapped in paper bands. People used to buy them in the Five-and-Dime to replace the broken ties in their school oxfords and summer sneakers. Today, shoelaces come in a large variety of colors and are sealed in a blister pack by machine in China or India. But back in the early-to-middle 1900s, women in southern New England, like Mama and her sisters, bound the laces with paper labels and got paid pennies per gross for 144 perfect pairs. They were known as "pairers" and Mama worked for over fifty years at this repetitive, mind-numbing job.

The instrument she used was a small reel that was attached to the table before her by a screw assembly such as the one on an old-fashioned meat grinder. Attached to the reel was a bar of steel from which three five-inch spikes projected, two at one end about an inch apart and the third at the other end. The inner spike had a slit about three inches deep. She lined up the aglets of two shoelaces (those fingernail like wrappings on each end), spun the reel to wrap the laces evenly on top of themselves, then touched the edge of a paper label to a roller floating in a small white porcelain tray of glue and wrapped the label around the laces. She pushed the first pair back on the pins and repeated this until four pairs had been lined up on the reel, then she slipped them off and placed them carefully in one end of a cardboard box. The process was repeated twice, each set of four being placed on top of the previous four. A wide band of paper, also edged with just the right amount of glue, bound the dozen together in a bundle. It was important not to put too much glue on the labels or wrappers to avoid getting it on the laces. This would make the item a "second" and the pairer was not paid for that mistake.

A dozen bundles fit in the box and this constituted a gross. The payment for each gross was fourteen to twenty-one cents, depending on the length of the laces. In the time it takes to describe this process, an experienced pairer like my mother could probably produce two or three dozen pairs.

Mama went to work at the Providence Braid company when she turned fourteen. Until she retired fifty-one years later, with four short time-outs to give birth to her children, this was my mother's world.

Mama made very few "seconds" but those that she did make found their way, along with odd lengths and leftovers, into her lunch bag and from there into a large cardboard carton in our attic. The ubiquitous "shoelace box" was a staple in my childhood and we found many uses for them in addition to replacing those we broke tying our shoes. To this day there is a small bag of laces tucked into my lower dresser drawer.

One summer toward the end of my freshman year in high school, Mama came home from work and told me that the company had gotten a new automatic pairing machine and that they were looking for someone to train who had never done pairing before.

"Nobody wants to take the time to learn this machine," she explained, "we'd lose too much money. I told them how smart you are, Lou, and that I thought you could learn this pretty fast, and they agreed to give you a summer job. They'll pay you twelve cents an hour to learn, but once you are up to speed you can go on a "piece-work" rate of fifteen cents a gross."

"But what about my job at the hospital?" I whined. "They said they were going to let me work in the main kitchen this summer, which means I could work full time."

The year I turned twelve, my friend Evelyn and I found after school jobs at Memorial Hospital delivering trays to patients. I was looking forward to a summer with my friends and afternoons between lunch and dinner when we could go swimming at the pond on the hospital grounds. I was appalled at the thought of working in a factory, especially with my mother.

"Oh Lou," Mama argued, "You can hardly make enough for carfare. This is a chance to make some real money and maybe keep the job part-time when you go back to school."

My only hope was that my father would support my staying on at the hospital. He had made it clear that all his children were to get an education so they would not have to work in the routine jobs such as he and my mother held in factories. Surely he wouldn't want me to work at The Providence Braid. I was shocked when he said, "Sounds like a good idea. You'll get a chance to see how hard your mother works in case you ever get any ideas that you don't want to go to college."

Not go to college? Why would he even think such a thing? It was all I ever knew since I was three. I felt betrayed but I never argued with Daddy. I'd watched my sister try this, and it always ended up with him angry and her crying, even though she sometimes got her way.

I was filled with dread and anxiety. I was also angry at the thought of spending hour after hour doing the same stupid job that my mother had been doing since she herself was fourteen. I thought that the fact that she could fill box after box with neatly paired shoelaces indicated a lack of intelligence. I felt too smart for this, but I could not say so.

As Mama and I entered the red brick building for the first time, the roar of the "braiders" was over-powering. The large machines occupied one end of an immense open space on the second floor. Clanging, clashing machine parts braided the thread as it spun off whirling bobbins. The machine then cut the braid to length and fed it into the "tipper" which applied the aglets.

At the far end of this vast room were lines of tables where the pairers sat in front of their reels. Each woman had her own personal instrument clamped to the edge of the table in front of her. Large open cartons filled with mounds of black, brown or white shoelaces surrounded each pairer so that no time was lost in reaching for the next pair. Grab, slide, spin, wrap, paste, over and over again. The twenty or thirty women were a blur of hands and laces and labels.

I sat at a table by myself in front of the new semi-automatic reel and was shown how to select two laces of identical length, slip them into the slot so that the machine could spin and apply the label automatically. Some efficiency expert had designed this to speed up the process. I don't remember exactly how it worked. I don't think I wanted to know. I do recall that the agility of the worker to feed the laces into the reel rapidly was important to making the process profitable. I also remember feeling clumsy, bored, lonely and stupid. Try as I might I just could not get the hang of grabbing two shoelaces from the large carton by my side, sliding the tips into the slot of the reel and holding them as the reel spun its measured turns to make a neat bundle. The braids slipped off each other, I put too much glue on the label and I felt like taking a break every few minutes.

I would glance at the other women seated near my mother and see the boxes of paired shoelaces stack up as if by magic. I don't recall how long I lasted, I'm sure it was not more than a week or two. I was let go and I felt relieved but I also felt like a failure and that I had let my mother down. I tried to convince myself it was because it was a stupid job and only stupid people could learn it. But I know my mother was embarrassed when I was fired. Her "smart" daughter could not even learn to pair shoelaces. At the time I was just glad that I would never become like my mother, a "pairer."

It would be many years before I understood the complexity of my mother and the reasons that kept her tied to this job. And it would be many years before I realized that her love and devotion to me bound us tighter than the glue she applied to endless numbers of labels, and was far stronger and more enduring than those tough brown and black laces that lay in tangled heaps by her side for fifty-one years as a "pairer." ■

On the Mend

"I'll be leaving in ten minutes, hon. Anything you need before I go?"

"Just shut the storm door so it latches. I don't want to have to get up and close it again."

"I'm sorry about that. I tightened the screw thingy, so I think it'll hold. I'll call someone in the morning to come fix it."

"All it needs is, you jiggle it after it shuts, to make it click into place. That's all it needs."

"I did do that, honey. But it's awful windy out. I guess it came loose."

"That's a good storm door. I got the heavy duty. It cost a pretty penny, but you wouldn't know about that."

"Well, I guess not. You always handled the money. I never did have a head for figures. I'll have someone come look at it."

"Now, that's just swell. Your solution to everything: If there's a problem, just throw more money at it. That'll take care of it. When did you become a Democrat?"

"Why, no such thing, darling. If you could fix it – I mean, if it can be fixed, I know you'll do it, when you're back on your feet. Speaking of feet, I've got to run. You sure there's nothing I can get you before I leave?"

"What's the big rush, for God's sake? Where are you off to, anyway?"

"I told you, honey. It's Helen and Bill's anniversary. Remember?"

"You mean to tell me you're going out in this weather? It's snowing like a son of a bitch. You are actually going to venture out in weather like this, to go drink that rot gut they buy by the gallon? And eat Ritz crackers and Cheez Whiz?"

"Why, honey, you were the one who accepted the invitation. Remember? Before your accident? I didn't want to go. Goodness knows, I still don't. I'd much rather stay home with you. But now you can't go, so I have to. All by myself. Besides, I'm bringing the cake. It's the kind you like, that orange mocha kind. There's a slice for you in the kitchen."

"Oh great. A slice of mine own. In the kitchen is it? I can just hobble out there and have me a feast."

"Sweetheart, you're supposed to exercise anyway. Dr. Oswald said you should get out of bed more often."

"Did Dr. Arsehole tell you what I'm supposed to use for legs?"

"Your walker's right here. And I put your cane out, too."

"Great. All that a man could wish for: a walker, a cane, and a piece of cake, while the little woman's out on the town."

"Don't get so excited, honey. Dr. Oswald said to avoid stress at all costs."

"How about avoiding the obscenely inflated cost of that quack's unsolicited, dubious professional opinion? Did he say anything about that? For the sake of sweet Jesus of Nazareth, tell me how to avoid that, will you?"

"Oh, honey, he's done you so much good. We're so lucky to have him. You're so much better. Really, really on the mend, darling. You just have to keep your spirits up. Eat regularly, get lots of sleep. How about I fix you a cup of tea before I leave? Here, let me plump those pillows. Scooch up. You can watch the news. Do you want Brian Williams or Katie Couric?"

"I'd like to watch someone beat Brian Williams to a pulp with Katie Couric, that's what I'd like."

"Okey-dokey. Here's the remote. You choose. I'll go turn the kettle on."

"What kind of witch's brew are you going to make?"

"You like that ginger-mango green tea. That would go nice with the cake."

"Is that dinner? Is that my honest to God repast?"

"Why no, silly. We'll eat later. I'll only be gone an hour. Or so. Goodness, I'm going to be late. I have to run."

"Only an hour. My God, how can somebody live with somebody for two frigging decades, without realizing he's on his frigging own, if he gets sick? If he gets injured. 'In sickness and health.' That's rich. That takes the cake."

"Oh, shoot. I keep forgetting the cake. I'll get you that slice right now. And maybe, instead of tea, a glass of wine? No, wait: some brandy. How about that? Cake and schnapps."

"Perfecto. 'Get the old boy swacked, and maybe he'll break his God damned neck, while I'm gone.' What, did you loosen the screws in the walker, too? Is there a banana peel on the floor?"

"Oh, I'm glad you reminded me. I'd better roll up that scatter rug in the hall, so you won't slip."

"Wasn't that part of your grand scheme? Liquor me up and hope the old crip falls and breaks his neck, all alone in the house."

"There, you lie still and I'll tuck you in. That better?"

"If you're planning on embalming me, you should have done it before wrapping me so tight. I can't breathe. You cut off my circulation. There won't be any body fluids to drain."

"Gracious, just look at the time. I'm off, sweetheart. I'll be back in an hour. Two at the most. I really must go. Ciao, darling. Kisses. I love you." ■

One-Way Transport

A U-Haul truck, empty, its doors still open, was parked in the field below the house when she drove home after work. From the road she could see, strewn along the driveway, across her dooryard and up onto the porch, piles of furniture and stacks of boxes, some of them spilling their contents: pots, pans, china and silverware; pillows, blankets, linens, clothing; books and magazines; tools and games. Leaning against the porch railing, a divan, two mattresses, and a throne-size gilded chair with a broken leg.

She recognized Vinny Vecchio down on the shore, next to the boat barn. Salvator had to be somewhere nearby, but he was nowhere to be seen. She wanted to keep on going, but where was she to go? The road dead-ended just beyond her property. And her dog, alert to the sound of the engine, was already crawling out from his hiding place under the porch. Was running down the hill toward her car. She stopped and opened the door. He scrabbled up across her lap and lay down on the passenger seat, his head on his paws. He would not look at her.

As she drove up to the house and parked, Salvator, wearing her bib apron over his bib overalls, appeared in the doorway, filling it, beaming. "Hee hee," he said, waving a soup ladle. Tomato paste splattered the clapboards. He was making spaghetti sauce to which, he explained as he came down off the porch and tacked toward the car, would be added the clams that he and Vinny were going to dig at low tide. "Hey, Vinny," he yelled out over the meadow, "there's clams down there. Free, no charge. Be my guest." Vinny could not have made out the words at that distance, but he waved to acknowledge the call, and turned back toward the water.

Lowering his voice to a whisper, Salvator leaned in through the open car window, explaining Vinny's presence, but not his own: Vinny was sad; Vinny'd had a fight with his wife; Vinny could not be left like that, so he, Salvator, invited Vinny along for the ride.

"It'll be a vacation for Vinny. He can take it easy, get a different slant on things."

And she could take it easy, too. Was she worried about something? She looked tired. She worked too hard. But that was about to change.

"Your old man's back, babes. With a very big deal in the works."

Not like the other times, those crumb jobs that fell through the cracks. This one was in the bag. You could take it to the bank. So, she could ease up, maybe quit her lousy job. With his tools and the rest of his stuff all in one place, he could finally get down to business. For now, though, he had to get back to his cooking.

"Repeat after me, sweetheart, 'Life is good.' And so's my spaghetti sauce."

He held the soup ladle to her mouth, so she might lick it.

"Not hungry yet? That's more for me, then. You want to walk down to the water, work up an appetite? Talk to Vinny for awhile, before supper? Kind of welcome him to our home. But don't say nothing about his wife. Don't tell him what I said, O.K.?"

The round head with its tight, black curls withdrew from the car window and then reappeared in it and kissed her above the ear. "I forgot to say I love you," Salvator said. "I'm a lucky man to have you in my corner."

He went back across the dooryard to an open crate stuffed with what appeared to be terry cloth bathrobes. He slipped the soup ladle into a tool loop on his overalls, hefted the crate on his shoulder, and leapt up the steps into the house.

She stayed in the car and prayed: Please, God, make him get out of my life. Make him be nonexistent to me, so I could never have known him, never have wakened sick with the knowledge that he was somewhere and was coming back. Please make my fingers stop wanting to touch his face. Erase the memory of his sweetness. Let him be an emptiness I do not know I carry within me, so I will not come to wish him dead, conjuring a phone call from a stranger with the news. Make him get back in the truck and drive down Passamaquoddy Road, over the bridge to the mainland, up the hill, past the sail loft and the berry factory and, by the time he has reached Elksport, I will have forgotten he ever was. And I will never ask for anything else again.

She let the dog out of the car and headed down toward the boat barn. As she came to the truck, she said, "Please God, don't let me look. It's none of my business. It's out of my hands."

She stopped at the open passenger door. In the cab, there were joints in the ashtray, seeds on the floor, beer in a cooler. She took two cans of beer and went on down to the shore.

Vinny accepted one of the beers, and they sat on the dock looking over at the mainland, not speaking. There was a slight chop on the water. Herring gulls, perhaps a dozen, waited in the shoals for the ebb tide to expose mussels clinging in clusters to the rocks beneath. The dog sniffed around the boat barn for awhile. Then he came up on the dock, lay down next to them, and went to sleep.

"This is a beautiful place you got here," Vinny finally said.

She was grateful to him for breaking the silence. They did not know each other well. She'd met him only once before, at Christmas, when Salvator's gift to her had been a trip to New York City.

"I'm sorry your wife couldn't come," she said, instantly regretting it.

"She'd like this," Vinny said. "She don't get out much." He turned away from her. She thought there might be tears in his eyes.

"I can't stay," Vinny said. "I got to get back. I didn't tell Sal, yet. He thinks I'm staying till Monday. But I'll be shoving off before dark. I'll drive the truck back."

She felt tired. She wanted to lie down on the ledge, the granite still warm from the sun, and go to sleep to the sound of waves sloshing through the rock weed.

"How're you holding up?" Vinny asked.

She shrugged.

"You didn't bargain for this, did you?"

"No," she said.

"Where are you going to put all his junk? Your house ain't that big."

"I don't know," she said.

"Look, I got to level with you: that ain't all you don't know. Sal's in bad shape. That drive up from Brooklyn was a crap shoot. I never seen him like that. Like the on/off switch in his head wasn't working right. Maybe I'm sticking my nose in where it ain't wanted, but I don't think you know what you're getting into. I think you're biting off more than you can chew."

"Since you bring it up," she said, "I didn't bite it off. It's being shoved down my throat."

"Wait a minute. Hold on. You didn't ask him to move in with you? Lady, please tell me I didn't just drive five hundred miles to help a buddy muscle in where he ain't wanted."

"We talked about it. A long time ago. But now, whenever he leaves, which is whenever he gets the urge, he says he won't be coming back. So, the answer to your question is, No."

"Ah, Christ. Excuse my French. I didn't know. Honest to God. I know the guy since second grade. I love him like a brother. But I never know what he's got up his sleeve. I didn't see him since you guys come over Christmas. Then, out of the blue, yesterday he calls me and asks for a hand moving. Next thing I know, I'm halfway the hell to Canada. How long has he been boozing like this?"

She shook her head.

"And he shouldn't be smoking so much dope. He can't handle it."

"I know," she said.

"Well, what do we do now?"

She thought of the rages that sometimes swelled in Salvator, ballooning his face, making his eyes small and blind. She thought of the all-night, one-man dialogues; the bottle on the table, broken glass on the floor, the dog hiding under the porch. She wanted to beg Vinny to talk to Sal. Take him back in the truck to the city. Make him see that she couldn't be in his corner anymore.

While Vinny talked to Sal, she would sleep on the granite ledge. When she woke up, the truck would be gone. The crushed grass where it had been would spring back. There would be no trace. Next year, she would think about having the field mown to make a proper lawn. With a flower bed, perhaps. She would prune the lilac bush and the apple trees, so there would be abundant purple flowers in the spring and apples, small and tart the way she liked them, in the fall. At twilight, she would call her dog, and they would walk to the Point to watch the sun go down. Then they'd walk home, and she'd go to bed and sleep through the night without dreaming.

"So, what are we going to do?" Vinny asked again.

"Nothing," she said. "We're going to go eat spaghetti."

They finished their beers and walked up toward the house. Salvator, picking wild flowers for the table, came to meet them in the meadow. He smiled at them, and handed each of them a daisy.

"I'm hungry," he said. "Let's skip the clams." ■

A Night at Gastroni's

It was a fancy nightclub dinner menu with an impressive wine list. The borders of cherubs and curlicues and the carefully articulated phrases, set in cursive fonts, projected a regal motif. As I was reading, mentally tasting the flavors inspired by the attractive descriptions, a large housefly alighted on the menu.

The insect, though bulky, confidently gripped the menu so that its back legs could rub each other. My attention was drawn to the iridescence of its black hairy body. The globed eyes looked like faceted rubies in my table's candlelight, and the wings were large and transparent enough for me to notice dark pipe-like veins that plumbed them. What, I thought, was such an unsavory creature doing in this esteemed establishment.

In a moment the housefly's wings buzzed into action. As it ascended, I could feel my menu get lighter. I saw it circle the next table, then fly on, not to scavenge from the other diners, but more to survey the scene. Elegantly dressed people at the tables ignored the insect, but I was fascinated as I watched this intruder make its way to the kitchen door, and, when a black-tie waiter pushed through with a tray, fly right in.

Unbelievable as it may seem, a housefly was about to change my life. It happened like this:

Several weeks later, on a summer afternoon, when the air was hot and still, I was outside reading an assigned text about the history of labor law. Despite my enthusiasm for the subject, I soon discovered that after the first chapter, which dwelt on 16th Century charters granted by kings, I was feeling drowsy. By the middle of Chapter Two: Trades, Crafts and Guilds, I was nodding off, and before I was aware of it, I fell asleep, snuggled against a broad tree and comforted in the fragrant grasses.

When I awoke, many padded claws were carrying me.

I could feel my body being transported along a dark tunnel. I struggled to sit upright, but soon realized I had no choice but to lie passively prone and await my fate. The tunnel was winding and climbing upward. Eventually, as the tunnel became wider and higher I began to see obscure ambient light. I noticed small rocks and roots embedded in the moist rough surfaces, which appeared to be passages excavated in compacted soil. The smell was earthy, but not unpleasant. It was silent.

Finally, I was brought into an open, cavernous chamber, where a single ray of light pierced the dark. In the brightest area there was an outsized russet-colored ant, with numerous smaller ants around it. I was carefully placed on my feet. This is when I realized that I was smaller than the large ant.

A few ants approached me and one gently tapped my head with its antenna. This didn't hurt, and I wasn't afraid. These ants retreated and I was left standing alone, confused and perplexed. Then another ant came to me. It was my size, and its mouth was shaped more like leathery lips than the others, whose mouths were hard-shelled and angular. When this ant moved its lips, I could hear squeaky sounds that I thought might be words although I couldn't recognize them. That ant retreated.

Another ant approached and held a mint leaf with a drop of amber liquid in it. The drop glistened in the beam of light. I guessed I was supposed to take the leaf, and when I smelled the drop, found it to be honey. As I sipped it, most of the ants turned and dispersed in the tunnels, leaving only the large ant and a few others. I stood there bewildered, looking around.

In a few minutes, the ant with the lips came back, carrying in its front legs a book. I could read its cover, *Formic to English Translation Dictionary*. The ant turned pages and paused on a page, then looked at me and made squeaky sounds again. This time, I could recognize the words, "I am Crusto, translator for the Inter-Species League. I have been summoned to communicate with you. Can you understand?"

I stared at this creature in disbelief. Before I could fully appreciate what was transpiring, I heard myself reply, "Yes, I can understand. But, I certainly don't understand! Where am I and what am I doing here?"

"You are in the main gallery of an ant colony. That is the queen. She wants me to assure you that you are safe. You will be made comfortable. Are you ready to go to a chamber that has been prepared for you?"

"Shall I bow to the queen?" I asked.

"No. The queen does not see. Please follow me."

I walked behind Crusto, and two other ants followed me. We proceeded through narrowing tunnels, descending deeper into the colony. Crusto stepped into an oval sphere, which had a litter of cedar sawdust in one area. The attendant ants remained in the tunnel while I joined Crusto.

"This will be your chamber while you are here. I will be nearby. The two ants outside will serve you. It is now time to rest. I hope you will be comfortable. If you need anything, alert the ants and they will summon me. I will return shortly."

"Before you depart, Crusto, I would like something to write with, a pencil and paper. I think best when I write."

"Perhaps some wasp paper, the juice of blackberry, and a barb for a quill. I will see to it."

Crusto tapped the head of each servant ant, and they both hurried off. I was now alone in a dark cave, and despite this uncertain situation, didn't feel threatened. As I said, it didn't hurt when that first ant tapped my head, and I didn't feel afraid now.

I thought about that summer afternoon, the tree and the labor book. Were they still there? Even though that was only hours ago, it seemed so far away. How could this drastic reduction to an ant colony have happened me? I lay on the sawdust and fell asleep.

Some time later, Crusto woke me. There was a nutshell bench in the chamber, and a lattice of twigs formed into a table. On the table was a sheaf of gray knobby papers, black ink in seedpods, and several bumble bee barbs. I saw that on the wall behind the table two Monarch butterfly wings had been mounted. They added vivid colors to the otherwise dim space. I thanked Crusto for his attentions.

"How shall I address you?" Crusto asked.

"I am Rocky." (Note to reader: That's not my real name. I figured that being in an ant colony where nobody knew me I could be called anything, and I've always wanted to be called Rocky.)

"Well then, Rocky, I have been summoned to translate and you may accompany me if you wish. We must leave now."

"Yes, I would love to. Can you tell me where we are going and what I should do?"

"The termites need to talk. Come."

I gathered a barb, took a sheet of wasp paper and one pod of juice, and followed Crusto through the tunnels. The two servant ants followed. It wasn't long before we were outside the colony. The night was warm, fresh-smelling after the not unpleasant odors of the colony. I had to run to keep up with Crusto who raced through stalks of grass that seemed like slender trees. We came at last to a column that appeared to me as a skyscraper, but was just a balsam fir. We climbed the uneven and sometimes sticky bark and eventually came to a smooth bare hole in the trunk.

What a sight to behold!

As I caught my breath from the exertions of the climb, I saw that we were in a large open space within the trunk. A cluster of lightning bugs hung suspended from above on a long spider silk. Forming a chandelier, they collectively provided a warming luminous hospitality.

On the inside walls of the tree were protrusions that formed little ledges. They were like tables. At each table were gathered two or more insects. I saw honeybees at one table, waggling their abdomens in little figure eights. Three glistening beetles quietly chewed a brown fiber at another. Two gaudy green Luna moths, one caressing a pupa, crowded around a larger table on the far wall. A party of crickets was bunched together, chirping a chorus.

Everywhere were small individual lightning bugs that were like waiters, attending the animated insects at their tables.

"This is where I am to meet the termites," said Crusto.

A lightning bug came to us and illuminated our way to a table where three menacing-looking termites were already waiting. The two servant ants that had accompanied us stayed at the entrance. I was given a tuft of soft thistledown to sit on. A lightning bug handed each of us a large sliver of mica with columns of written characters, none of which I recognized. I took it for a menu.

Crusto stood next to the largest termite who was almost transparent and had no eyes. The two others were smaller and reddish. Crusto tapped the head of the large termite and the termite tapped Crusto's head. Crusto turned to me and said, "This is Brank, queen of her termite colony. She wishes you to be made comfortable. She will not mind if I translate to you."

Crusto and Brank then tapped each other. The other two termites held their antennae, each of which looked like a string of pearls, to Brank's head, so they could follow the conversation.

Again, I gazed upon the larger scene. Everywhere I looked insects were engaged in what appeared to be intimate conversations. I took a sheet of the wasp paper, opened the pod of black juice, and began to verbally sketch the scene with the bee's barb. The insects fascinated me with their beautiful colors and variety of shapes. The eyes of the creatures at the next table, for instance, a group of fleas, were intelligent-looking, as each individual focused upon one, who apparently was the speaker. A damselfly came to us. Crusto tapped a bit. The damselfly rushed away and Crusto said to me, "I have ordered nectars and asked for the proprietor to come by. I want you to meet him."

Soon a loud buzzing heralded an enormous hairy housefly, who landed on the mica menu, gripping it with his front legs and rubbing his rear legs, very much like the housefly I had so recently met at the fancy nightclub.

This housefly greeted the termites and Crusto with a noisy acknowledgment gesture. Turning to me he buzzed and moved his antennae. Crusto translated to me very proudly and according to some formal protocol, "Welcome to Gastroni's! I am himself, Gastroni. Tonight we are honored to have you here with the Termite Queen. We also have many celebrities at the other tables.

Gastroni's, you know, serves the royalty of Class Insecta." Gastroni preened his legs and waited for some adoring response.

I stopped my note taking, stood up straight, bowed at the waist and said, "I am so honored to meet you, Gastroni. This is a magnificent establishment."

Gastroni moved his jewel-like eyes and noisily lifted himself off the menu. This gesture was exactly like my first encounter with a housefly.

Lightning bugs brought the nectars while Brank and Crusto conversed. Every now and then, one of the other termites tapped Crusto's head and Crusto tapped back.

There came a pause. The termites sipped their nectars; Crusto did too.

I resumed writing a description of these events, which is what you are reading. I cannot adequately express the curious feelings I experienced being at Gastroni's. It was wonderful to be so close to these creatures for whom I had never felt anything but mild dislike. Now, they seemed enchanting, and I was eager to know more about them. The three termites I was looking at were especially magnetic. The mouthparts were shaped like scythes and looked fearsome, while, at the same time, they also appeared vulnerable and timid. I looked forward to having Crusto educate me about this exotic new miniature world.

"The situation is this," said Crusto. "The termites inhabited a pier by the harbor. During a storm, it was destroyed and washed away, into the sea. Wait a moment."

One of the red termites tapped Crusto's head again.

"That termite said that there were many other occupants in the pier. Red worms burrowed below the water, and termites had the dry part, above. Usually they didn't even see each other. But, with the storm and the water, everything was mixed up."

"The pier was turning in every direction as it floated. Termites were being dunked. Some were drowned. All the termite tunnels were flooded. The termites, as well as the worms, were terrified."

"Brank says that each of her sweet subjects felt that they were the captain. Each termite swiveled a splinter of wood as a tiller to steer the sinking pier. As the pier pitched and rolled in the storm, each individual at his station feared that he, and only he, failed his beloved queen by being a poor pilot. Brank asked me what had she done to deserve this punishment for her entire colony?"

Just then the buzzing noise and Gastroni arrived with a damselfly who delivered more nectars and a nutshell of aphids. With a loud flapping of his wings and his hairy legs dangling, Gastroni took off to another table, alighting on their mica menu.

The termites and the ant milked their respective aphids and sipped their nectars.

Soon the termites arose and crawled back to the entrance of Gastroni's and departed. I asked Crusto what he had told them. He said in his squeaky voice, "Brank should have announced to each termite to steer their tiller (and therefore, the floating pier) in a single direction. There could only be one captain. I couldn't tell Brank that it made no difference which direction they should point. As long as every individual pointed her tiller in the same direction, the one given by Brank, each termite would believe it was the best course. The idea that a random storm might cause such destruction is beyond Brank's understanding. Brank just knows that the storm happened because she had done something terrible and this was the punishment. I tried to calm her by saying that everything would soon be back to normal."

Crusto resumed tasting the nectar, then said, "I have come to believe that the whole insect world is an enigma, a harmless enigma that is made terrible by the mad attempt to interpret it as though it had an underlying truth."

I made notes of what Crusto had just said. Crusto and I were quiet at the table, enjoying the nectars (I didn't much care for aphids). Suddenly, the loveliest diaphanous lacewing flew over and caressed Crusto. There was much tapping.

Before I became ant-sized, I had never really appreciated insects. Now, since I could see this lacewing's amazingly fine filigree tracery on her slender and streamlined gossamer wings, I experienced an awareness of her as wondrous and beautiful. When I closely observed this delicate, exciting individual, I felt some romantic attachment that I could not really comprehend. Her scent was overpowering and delicious to me. I just knew that I would have to see her again.

Later, on our return to the ant colony, I confessed to Crusto my infatuation with the lovely lacewing. He promised to arrange a meeting at Gastroni's soon.

I also recalled to Crusto my experience at the nightclub when a large housefly settled on my menu there and how its back legs cleaned each other before it flew off in a similarly proprietary way.

"Oh, of course Rocky, you wouldn't know it, but there is a Gastroni's in every town. In fact, Gastroni's is a franchise operation. Quite a little operator is our Gastroni." ■

Thanks to Umberto Eco for his thought-provoking words.

Bongo's Back

She was leaving to catch a plane for Cape Town. The hotel phone rang, jarring her last-minute preparations. *Who could be calling at this hour of the morning?* She picked up the receiver gingerly.

"Carol?" Louder still, "CAROL?"

"Yes. Who's this?" A scowl formed on her weathered face as she strained to hear.

"It's Robert."

Her housemate half a world away in California sounded apologetic.

"Robert? Is that you?" Carol gripped the phone. "What's up?" She sat down on the bed. Surprise calls from home when she was working abroad made her nervous.

"It's Bongo. The people who adopted him are here."

"You've got to be kidding." She sighed. "Why the sudden visit?"

"They want to return him. The lady is a wee bit upset," he related. "Says you didn't tell her he had a back problem."

"Back problem? A dog? That's a helluva twist! Let me talk to her."

It was the newlyweds. They had taken a fancy to the Tibetan terrier mix she'd temporarily sheltered in a soft moment. It had ended up in her backyard one late afternoon, curled up under a Japanese maple at the far end of the lawn. She'd taken the mutt for a wet string mop, the kind her mother used to wield, until he raised his head. The smell of damp, slightly sour fur gave him away as she approached his hiding place. Umber eyes, peeking out from under a fringe of stiff bangs, mirrored the look of a child caught with one hand in a candy jar. Looking up, he half wagged his sodden tail. There was no sign of a collar.

As Carol reached down to pat him, the muddy pup turned over in supplication. Her heart melted. She coaxed him out to the lawn and scratched his ear for several moments, talking to him as if he were a toddler. He licked her arm in friendship. Then she caught him between her legs, turned on the hose and gave him a good scrubbing. It did wonders. Once he'd shaken and dried himself on the lawn, the little terrier emerged fluffy white as a down pillow. Carol made a spontaneous decision to give him a safe haven until his owner—if he had one—materialized. She should have taken the dog right to a shelter.

Bongo, as she dubbed him, turned out to be a chewer with a Kleenex fetish. No wastebasket in her house was safe. And she caught him more than once grabbing hold of a wayward thread on the end of her Turkish carpet, teasing it into unraveling. Still, Bongo was an engaging little character with his floppy bangs and curly upright tail.

Carol's peripatetic life as an international consultant had dictated that if no one came forward, after she'd posted flyers and an advert in the local paper, she'd best take Bongo to the Humane Society and move on.

She'd waited three weeks to hear a response. Nothing.

On an overcast day just before she was about to fold and take Bongo to the pound, she'd put on her trainers and set out for a last run with the dog along the path that skirted Phoenix Lake. They'd crossed the bridge and were heading down through the redwood trees when a young couple appeared from the opposite direction.

"What an adorable dog," the lanky, twenty-something blond called. "What kind is he?"

Carol stopped. "I think he's a Tibetan terrier. He sort of adopted me. I'm not sure." She pulled on Bongo's leash and made him sit at the edge of the path, out of the way of joggers and hikers.

The girl looked as if she'd popped out of a 1950s movie, pageboy in place and a dash of neon-pink lipstick. Her tanned, athletic partner wore a dark blue UC baseball cap, gray sweats and tennis shoes. He followed her across the dusty path to have a closer look at Bongo.

"We love animals," the girl beamed, leaning down to pat the dog's topknot. Bongo wiggled his curly tail in ecstasy as she looked up at her partner.

The man nodded with a desultory grin and bent down to give the terrier's spiky head a tousle. "How long have you had him?"

"About three weeks. He was abandoned." Carol watched the two of them with Bongo. They seemed like nice people, the kind of animal enthusiasts who might do rescue work.

"You want him?" She asked, making a snap decision. "No one has responded to notices I've posted and I travel a lot. I can't keep him. In fact, I was about to take him to the pound."

"Oh no!" The girl exclaimed passionately, her lower lip turned down.

"We just got married," her husband interjected. Something about his angular frame reminded Carol of the Tin Man in *The Wizard of Oz*. "And we already have three cats." He was eyeing his wife as she scratched Bongo's ear.

The girl smiled up at him. "I wonder how he'd get along with the cats?"

Carol didn't want to speculate.

"He *is* a funny little runt," her husband observed, his eyes brightening. "But with the cats..." He looked at his wife and raised one eyebrow meaningfully.

"That's okay," Carol assured them. "I'll find someone. Let's go, Bongo."

She left the couple and continued down the trail with the little dog bouncing along at her side. Disappointment that her pitch hadn't worked nagged her. *What am I going to do with you, dog? What am I going to do, damn it?*

They'd gone a quarter mile, dodging runners and strollers, when Carol heard frantic voices calling from behind, "Hey, wait. We want to talk to you. Wait up."

She turned round to see the newlyweds running to catch up.

"We decided we might want him, but we need a few days to think about it," the man burst out, catching his breath. "What's your name and telephone number?"

Carol supplied the information with some misgiving. "I was going to take him to the Humane Society tomorrow, but I could hold off for a couple of days. I'd need a decision by Wednesday at the latest. I'll be leaving for South Africa on Saturday," she warned.

Over the next few days, she answered phone calls from the husband or wife about Bongo's diet, shots and health with careful patience. The couple still seemed unsure. By Wednesday she'd given up and was collecting Bongo's gear together when the phone rang. It was the husband.

"We'll take him," he announced. "I just hope he gets used to the cats."

Carol breathed deeply, relieved that the couple had come to a decision. She didn't want to see the dog end up at the pound. "I'm so glad," she said. "You'll love Bongo. He's one of a kind. Can I bring him over this evening?"

"I guess so. Say about 6:30?"

"I'll be there." After hanging up the receiver, she shouted, "Hallelujah," waving her arms skyward and doing a little jig around the room.

She'd delivered the dog, his bowls and bag of dry food to the couple's modest two-story brick house on a tree-lined street. Having seen their home, Carol felt Bongo would be in good hands. She'd spent a few moments with him in his new digs, then left. She could turn her attention to the demands of the upcoming trip. It involved an assessment of the South African government's new health care program and required all her energy as she and her evaluation team flew around the country talking to people.

Now, a month later in Johannesburg, here was Bongo's new owner on the phone, prickly with irritation. "You didn't tell us Bongo had a back problem," the woman said. "We took him to the vet. They did an X-ray and told us his spine is out of alignment."

"I didn't *know* he had a back problem," Carol countered. She felt herself getting defensive, impatient. Bongo was the furthest thing from her mind. She had to join the rest of the team at the Jo-burg airport to catch the 8:30 plane to Cape Town. It was getting late.

"What happened?" She asked carefully.

"He was chasing our cats up the stairs. Somehow he threw his back out."

"You're kidding!" It was all Carol could do to nip the giggles bubbling up as an image materialized of Bongo bounding up stairs on his stubby legs in pursuit of three cats nearly his size.

"Well, we don't want a dog with a bad back!" The woman was irate. "You didn't tell us. I don't see how we can keep him."

Carol took a deep yoga breath and continued evenly, "Let me talk to Robert." She eyed her watch. "I won't be home for another four weeks."

Robert had been her renter and housemate for six months. Middle-aged and mild in temperament, he hailed originally from Wales. He found his way to the San Francisco Bay Area working as an accountant for a high tech firm. Recently, however, he'd decided to trade in the harried life of a numbers-cruncher for that of a masseur. He would live longer; the new vocation stood to feed his soul and it would put the hassles of Route 101 behind him.

He and Carol had fallen into an easy friendship with plenty of space to themselves. They shared dinners when Carol was in town. When she was gone, Robert held things together.

Calm as ever, Robert came on the line now. "Problem? Look, why don't you let them leave him with me. I'll see what I can do for the little rascal."

"Really? You sure you're not smoking something, Robert?"

He laughed. "Why not?"

"Thanks a million," Carol said. "I'll make it up to you."

"How's the job going?"

"It's going well. We still have a lot of interviews to do in Cape Town and Durban. I've got to meet my South African teammates at the airport, so I'd better get cracking."

"Don't worry about Bongo, luv. I'll take care of him," Robert finished.

Off and on, over the next few days, as Carol interviewed township dwellers and primary health care workers, she found images of Bongo bouncing up to meet her at the end of the day. Was the dog still in pain? How was Robert coping? Bongo was not a lie-about.

Then she forgot about them in the immediacy of her work with the assessment team.

When Carol arrived home, limp from the marathon trip between Johannesburg and San Francisco, Robert, his pale blue eyes mischievous, greeted her at the door with a crooked smile. He stooped down to pick up her suitcase. "How was the trip?"

"Not bad," Carol said, reaching up to hug him. "How did things go here?" She looked around for Bongo, dreading the sight of him limping about. "Where's Bongo? In the backyard?"

"No."

"What do you mean? Don't tell me you took him to the pound?"

"Not likely." He stalled for effect. "I be the bearer of good news," he said impishly. "Bongo's back problem is behind him. He's with his new family—the newlyweds. They came and got him. All's well that ends well." Robert carried her suitcase to the hall.

"I don't believe it!" she sputtered. "What happened? Tell all."

Taking off her shoes and jacket, Carol made for the kitchen to get a drink of water.

Robert followed her. Leaning his six-foot frame against a counter while Carol got down a glass and filled it, he confided nonchalantly, "After they left that day, I took Bongo out to the backyard and let him sniff around for a bit. He did seem in some pain. I let him settle down on the patio before I made friends with him again. After a while I lifted him up on the picnic table—very carefully, like he was fine China."

"What for?" Carol was trying to follow his drift while she staved off fatigue. Her head felt light. It was 2 A.M. in Johannesburg.

"I stretched him out on his tummy," Robert continued, "and began massaging his back—very gently. I thought he would protest, growl a little, but he liked it. Settled right down. I worked on him for nearly an hour. That dog got the royal treatment!" Robert smiled beatifically. "When I put him down on the patio again, he seemed a lot better. I repeated the massages a couple of times a day."

Carol laughed as an image of Robert as a doggie masseur took hold.

"It worked," he countered. "I continued the treatment for several days until Bongo seemed his normal self again. Then I called the newlyweds and told them how I'd solved his back problem. They were speechless. Came and got him."

Carol looked dubious, eyebrows raised.

"They seemed pleased to see him. Maybe they felt a little guilty about dumping him on me. The woman dropped to her knees and talked to him like he was a long-lost son, then she scooped him up in her arms. He gave her a nice, wet kiss on the chin. I guess they really did want him. I haven't heard from them since."

"Sounds like you've found your calling, Robert." Carol giggled. "Glad to hear they had a change of heart." ■

Early Morning Scramble

Gerri lies in bed, looking up at the pale blue ceiling, trying to reconstruct the leftovers of a dream. It troubles her. Two men—dressed like twins in plaid shirts and khakis; they were government types, talking as if she didn't exist and making plans for some sort of body heist to a foreign country.

Ordinarily, Gerri Baker is an adventuresome type living the way she does at the top of a lonely hill in the rocky woods. But in the dream, she was powerless as a pickle; tied to an iron bed with her arms and feet bound, two creeps plotting to transport her God knows where.

Now, Gerri bolts upright in bed, trying to shake herself free of the horrifying nightmare. The scene still haunts her. She swings her legs over the side and wiggles into worn felt slippers.

In the kitchen, she flips on the coffeemaker. Its red light blinks at her. A bubbling, honking noise follows as the Braun exhales bursts of steam. The enigmatic whistle has a soothing effect. Gerri wraps her tired bathrobe more tightly around her to stave off the dawn chill. The smell of brewing coffee is reassuring.

Looking out the back door window, she reaches for a carton of milk in the fridge. Out of the corner of her eye she catches a glimpse of something black as it trundles past her back stoop. Without her glasses on it's hard to know what the thing is, except that its dimensions alarm her.

Gerri dashes into the breakfast nook and grabs her specks from the clutter on the table in time to see a hefty animal, bigger than a St. Bernard, coming into view just outside the picture window.

"My God. It's a bear!" Breathless, she is awed by its bulk. The joy of seeing a sizable animal in the wild metastasizes into a nervous chill as it hits her that a windowpane is the only thing separating her from the omnivore.

The bear freezes as he catches sight of the white-haired woman behind the window. His black fur glistens with raindrops. He scans her with intense brown eyes. Satisfied that she is imprisoned by glass he continues meandering around to the deck side of the house.

Rushing to the door facing the deck, Gerri throws her body against it, making sure it's shut tight. Her mouth is dry. The trespasser outside swings his enormous head back and forth; then skirting the deck, he lumbers awkwardly over granite boulders and rocks.

Gerri runs into the bedroom to fetch her camera before realizing that it's out of film. "Damn. Mick and Handy would have gotten a kick outta that." She wishes her grandsons could see the brute. They'd be impressed.

Through the corner window she sees the bear rounding her house and navigating the driveway's piles of dirt left from a construction project. He makes it to the other side and heads down to the compost pile. A timber pole for aerating the decomposing mixture protrudes from the heap.

Clumsily, the brute climbs over a log form holding the compost pile together. With a swipe of his paw he smacks over the pole and begins nosing around in the damp cover of rotting leaves.

Gerri notices that his hind end resembles a giant panda all fluffed out while his front end is more streamlined, nose and all. She opens the window and yells, "Hey! Leave my compost alone! What are you looking for anyway?"

The bear, whose nose is buried in fermenting bliss, raises his shaggy head and rotates toward her. "I'm looking for suet and birdseed," he grunts.

Surprised, Gerri calls back, "You're not going to find any of that around here. I don't even have a bird feeder."

The bruin continues to rummage in the rotting compost. "Nothing but old lettuce, onion skins and coffee grounds," he growls. His haunches shimmy as he shakes off a deluge of rain from the spruces above. He's about to exit when Gerri remembers her dream.

"Wait a minute. I do have something."

The bear gazes at her, his curiosity aroused.

"I've got a couple of fat government men I could give you."

In disbelief, the animal scratches his furry head against a log.

"Wait. You'll see." With that, Gerri reaches into the recesses of her early-morning dream, grabs the two agents and hauls them out. She chases them into the kitchen and out the back door.

"There. That takes care of that," she smiles to herself, slamming the door shut.

The men stand on the porch, rubbing their eyes, shocked at their new surroundings. Suddenly, they spy the bear. He looks up to see two chubby men in plaid shirts and smells their delicious fear.

Tumbling after each other, the agents jump off Gerri's porch and hightail it into the woods.

That big, black bear lumbers after them in an ungainly sideways gait, his posterior doing a sort of hula while his front end and nose focus on hot pursuit.

The frantic duo disappears into the dense thicket, never to be seen again.

And the bear? That's a different story. ■

Jean Davison

Buried by Sand

I am the moss, clinging to jagged rocks
On a hillside above the big house.

I am the fir seedling nestled in the cracks
Of a torn stump on the once-wooded slope,

A lily, coral bells struggling,
In a grandmother's forgotten garden.

I am one blade of grass among many, crushed
By a torrent of sand where rabbits once nibbled.

I am a pebble without problems,
Flung from the porch by a playful child,

A stubborn spruce, torn by my roots
From a niche hugging the road's edge.

Smothered by wave after wave of sand,
We, who cannot speak, yet see and feel,
Lie buried, like the ancient cedars
At the well in Timbuktu — irreplaceable.

Jean Davison

Equinox Receding

The moon's fullness slips away.
Darkness captures another day-lit hour,
Reminder of our earth-bound position.
Balance, for a fleeting season,
Gives way to … imbalance.

The ceaseless heartbeat of the Earth,
A thousand mocassins on Hopi soil
Celebrate the return of fickle rain,
Their cadence echoes through my soul,
Quieting, confirming, persistent.

The solitary monarch in her time,
Casts shadows in a slow dance of death,
Burnt umber wings etched in black.
Does she grieve in flight, her mortality,
Or rejoice in the final act of creating?

It is a time of folding wings,
Retreating to a quiet shelter
Where summer reflections compete
With the shade of introspection.

Weather worn rocks, fingers of seaweed,
Ebb and flow of tides tug at my body,
Ocean spray crystallizing on my face
Or is it tears I taste?

It is a moment to stand naked in the sun,
Listening, hearing. *Ni ndigua.**
As the Earth shifts once more in her orbit.

*A Kikuyu phrase from Africa meaning, "I hear, I understand."

Survivors
(with thanks to Rachel Carson)

The storm from the east brings
its final waves of destruction
to the ravaged shore where I sit
watching the first shreds of dawn
caress the horizon. Last night I saw
fireflies flung through the air,
doomed and helpless, still sending
their primordial, longing signals into
the dark. All night the wind raged,
warm over the Chesapeake and strong,
changing its voice from the crashing
of waves to the shredding of
sweet gum leaves and a wistful hiss
as it passed through the bamboo grove,
stripping it bare. Today, at first light,
ospreys are soaring.

The Blessing

"Mother, make Betty stop singing!" my brothers would plead when we were growing up. But I couldn't stop. My head was full of songs; I remembered the melody line and lyrics from almost every song I had ever heard. What they found even more exasperating was the fact that I felt compelled to provide a musical response to any situation that arose. I learned to control the urge as I grew into adulthood because I didn't want to annoy people. I wasn't sure whether this talent was a curse or a blessing but I always hoped that some day I would find a use for it.

That day came one hot summer afternoon at a wedding reception in South Philadelphia. When bandleader Bob Mitchell asked me to sing with his orchestra at Antonio's Restaurant he told me the event was an important wedding reception. The fifteen band members were to dress in semi-formal attire: black suits, white shirts, and red ties. I was to wear a cocktail dress or evening gown.

This was big! Maybe the chance to break into the lucrative wedding circuit. I decided it was time for a change in my professional image. I was singing in jazz clubs at the time but dressing for club gigs involved little more than wearing a blouse instead of a tee shirt with my jeans and putting on eye makeup and lipstick. I had bought a petal pink floor-length gown on sale at Marshall's hoping for just such an occasion, and I set myself to the task of transforming a forty-plus housewife into a glamorous chanteuse. With the help of Clairol, I lightened my dark blonde hair to a Marilyn Monroe platinum and bought a raspberry wine lipstick and matching nail polish. Before my regular gig on Thursday night, I applied dark eyeliner and two shades of shadow, fluffed up my newly blonde tresses and put on a pair of spandex pants and a low-cut silver lamé blouse. A pair of strappy high-heeled sandals and a gold ankle chain completed the transformation. After a few tentative steps on the high heels, I managed to walk without falling on my face.

When I strutted into the club, Stan, the piano player and Tom, the drummer, whistled. Dante, the bass player, stared at me, speechless. The guys told me I sounded really good that night. I was convinced my new look had a lot to do with it. I was ready for the big time.

The day of the wedding dawned hot and sunny. I spent the morning getting ready. In the shower, I ran through the scales to loosen up my vocal chords. I blow-dried my hair and applied a large mound of mousse to give it body. I trimmed my toenails and painted them to match my raspberry red fingernails.

Applying enough makeup to keep from looking washed out under bright lights without looking clownish in natural light is an art, and that day I used all the artistic skill I could muster. My mirror told me I had succeeded: I was gorgeous. I stepped carefully into the pink gown and put on my most expensive rhinestone jewelry. The previous Christmas my mother-in-law had given me a pair of white opera gloves that had been a source of both amusement and mystery at the time. They were a perfect finishing touch.

Our instructions were to be at Antonio's at three o'clock. Antonio's is a restaurant in the Italian neighborhood of South Philadelphia famous for its authentic Italian food and elaborate décor. The only distinguishing feature of the exterior of the large green building was the red carpeted front entry, covered with a red awning bearing the restaurant's logo, so I was not prepared for the opulence of the lobby. Red was the predominant color. Red velvet sofas flanked by marble topped tables sat on plush red carpeting. Floor to ceiling marble Greco-Roman style columns flanked the reception area. Flamboyant floral arrangements sat on pedestals between the columns. It was blissfully air-conditioned.

In the rear of the enormous dining room was a serving area where elaborately decorated tables held platters of hors d'oeurves and wine colored punch flowed in a continuous stream from the penis of a statuette of a little boy. A tuxedo-clad maitre d' supervised a platoon of waiters in crisp white dinner jackets and waitresses in black dresses with white organdy aprons. They bustled about setting rows of long tables covered with white tablecloths with glistening crystal, china and silver, and placing decanters of red wine at intervals on the tables. The bandstand faced the tables and to the right of the dance floor sat the head table decorated with velvety red roses surrounded by white baby's breath.

Bob was already there, resplendent in his black suit, setting up music stands with the band's name and logo painted in gold letters on the front.

"Wow! " I exclaimed. "How many people are coming to this reception?"

"I believe the function manager said there will be six hundred guests," Bob said.

"Six hundred! Whose wedding is this anyway?" I inquired, thinking it must be the daughter of some high-level politician.

Bob said in a low voice, "All the function manager told me is that the father is a big wheel in Atlantic City. I thought it best not to ask too many questions."

I got his message. It was disappointing that this wasn't going to be my break into the society wedding circuit, but I knew the pay would be better than usual. The Mafia had a reputation for outdoing each other with lavish spending. I went out to the lobby where some of the band members had gathered to have a last cigarette and observed the guests as they arrived. With their lavishly bejeweled women by their sides, the men, wearing black tuxedos with pleated shirt fronts, red cummerbunds and bow ties, paraded in. Their black wavy hair, some streaked with silver, was styled *a la* Tony Curtis. They remained in the lobby clustered around a distinguished looking white-haired gentleman while their wives and girlfriends, after fixing me with a suspicious glare, headed *en masse* for the ladies' room.

"That's the Don," Stan whispered in my ear. Yes, I thought, he does look like a Godfather. He was tall and slender with swarthy skin and shaggy white eyebrows the same color as his meticulously styled hair. His tux and Italian loafers were clearly not from a rental agency. The men around him listened attentively as he punctuated his sentences with a flash of tanned hands ringed with gold and diamonds, a gold bracelet on his right wrist and a Rolex watch on his left.

As I watched, fascinated, I leaned against one of the pedestals and felt it move. I was shocked to discover it wasn't marble at all, but molded plastic. On closer inspection I saw that the floral arrangement on top was also plastic.

Disillusioned, I headed backstage where the musicians were beginning to tune their instruments. Bob had assembled the best, and some of the most colorful talent available for this event. Most had been on the road with name bands and were back in Philadelphia because they were road weary. Stan came out of Count Basie's band. Joe Brown, the tenor sax player, had played in Stan Kenton's band. He said he left because he was tired of playing music charts with so many notes that it looked like flies had pooped all over the paper. Barry, the alto sax player, had just come off tour with Woody Herman. Ferg, the drummer, was with Tommy Dorsey. The exception was Dante, an excellent bass player who never went on the road because his wife wouldn't stand for it. Dante had nine (or was it eleven?) children and said proudly that they would have had more if his wife hadn't used up all her eggs.

We waited there for Bob's signal then filed out to take our assigned places on the stage. My place was to the right of the bandstand in what the musicians referred to as the "canary chair." The band was in fine form. The first set consisted of quiet instrumentals that provided background music for the dinner. Because the vocalist does not normally sing during this set, I had the leisure to study the occupants of the head table. To the bride's right were the maid of honor, six bridesmaids, and an older woman I assumed was her mother. To her left were the groom and his attendants. The elegant white-haired man I had seen in the lobby sat at the end nearest the bandstand and next to him was a man who looked like a younger version of the older man. Bob identified them as the father and grandfather of the bride. The grandfather sat quietly observing the proceedings, but the father was never still, moving among the guests like a lord, wine glass in hand, flirting with the women and slapping the men on the back.

The Blessing

After the dinner was served and the tables cleared, the usual wedding rituals were observed and the dance set began. As the guests crowded onto the dance floor, the only person left sitting at the head table was the grandfather. Many in the party stopped to speak to him, but he seemed disinclined to engage in extended conversations.

When Bob announced the vocal selections and the band began to play the introductions, I would get up and walk to one of the microphones set up at the front of the bandstand. After the song was finished, I would go back to my chair. Throughout the evening the grandfather watched the dancers during the instrument segments but turned to face the band while I was singing. As we were ending the third set, I saw the bride's father approaching the stage. He called up to Bob.

"My father wants to hear *Half As Much*," he shouted.

Bob jumped down from the stage and stood next to the man. His six-foot-six frame seemed to shrink next to the shorter man and beads of perspiration formed on his brow.

"Gee," he said apologetically. "We would be happy to, but we don't have a chart for that song."

"Chart!" the man snorted. "What do you need a chart for? Just play it."

"I don't think the musicians know it," Bob stuttered.

I decided to come to his rescue. I walked to the edge of the stage and cleared my throat to get their attention. "I know that song," I said. "If Stan will accompany me, I'll be glad to sing it for your father."

The father gave me a wide grin and a thumbs-up, then headed back into the crowd. Bob stared at me, a worried look on his face. "I don't think that's such a good idea. Don't you think it's going to sound awfully thin with just the two of you?"

"It'll be all right," I assured him. I filled him in on the details of the song. It had been a popular country song that became a hit for Rosemary Clooney when she recorded it in 1951, one of the many I sang to torture my brothers. I trusted Stan; he was a skilled improviser. There was an old upright piano backstage and, concealed from the guests by a red velvet curtain, we quietly worked out the changes. By time for the next set to begin, we were ready.

When the band came back onstage, Bob announced, "We're going to start this set with a request from the bride's grandfather. Betty, our lovely vocalist, will sing *Half As Much*, accompanied by our fine pianist, Stan Gray."

He took the microphone off the stand and handed it to me so that I could stand close to the piano. Instead, I walked to the front of the stage and stood facing the grandfather. Stan played the introduction and I started to sing.

If you loved me half as much as I love you.

The old Don listened intently, his dark eyes focused on my face.

You wouldn't worry me half as much as you do.

He set the wine glass down on the table and leaned toward me. One by one the other musicians joined in: first Dante on bass, then Tony on drums.

You're nice to me when there's no one else around.
You only build me up to let me down.

To my amazement, tears glistened in the old man's eyes.

If you missed me half as much as I miss you.
You wouldn't stay away half as much as you do.

I hadn't thought about the meaning of the lyrics before.

I know that I would never be this blue.
If you only loved me half as much as I love you.

By the time we finished the first chorus, the band was beginning to swing hard, as impromptu performances sometimes do. Couples came onto the dance floor, but this time the grandfather's attention remained on the band. Bob looked ecstatic as Joe McCarthy played a solo so tender it raised goosebumps on my arms and made me glad I had decided to wear the opera gloves. The lead alto sax followed with one even sweeter and then Stan took a chorus. By the time he finished, the dancers had stopped dancing to listen.

As I sang the last chorus, I looked out at the old Don and saw him wipe tears from his cheeks with a white handkerchief. When the song ended the audience burst into applause. After we took our bows, the band returned to its scheduled program and I returned to my chair. Suddenly, the bride's father burst through the crowd, bounded onto the stage and walked over to where I was sitting. He reached down and lifted me out of the chair. He kissed me—hard—on the lips, then sat me back in the chair and leaped back down off the stage.

I sat there, stunned, my cheeks burning. I didn't dare look at the guys in the band but I knew they were struggling to keep a straight face. I would be in for a ribbing for a long time. It didn't matter. I had found a use for my talent and a nostalgic old Don had declared it a blessing. ■

How Much?

"How much?" The woman shouted from across the yard, waving a coffee mug above her head.

"Fifty cents."

"Too much. How about a quarter?"

"Sure, *whatever*." It was almost noon, and Donna no longer cared how much things went for — just that they went.

The yard sale wasn't supposed to begin until 9:00, but people started arriving as early as 7:45 and at the sound of the first car's crunching tires in the driveway, Ralph pushed his chair back from the table. "I'm outta here," he announced, slipping into his old, green windbreaker with Jacobsen's Engine Repair stitched on its back.

Car doors slammed outside, and Donna heard the women's excited voices. She, too, rose from breakfast and went outside to tell them to come back at 9:00. The morning had raced along from there, and now it was almost time to close up.

She gave the yard a once-over. It looked like an invading army had ransacked the house, leaving only the undesirables behind. A broken step ladder lay by the rosebush. The floor lamp that had been in her mother's living room since before Donna was born, stood over a box of romance novels that she knew would end up on the town dump. Even at 10 cents apiece, they were too far gone for anyone to want.

Surveying these rejects, then the cloudless, blue sky, Donna sighed. There are more important things than this junk, she thought, and immediately felt a twinge of guilt. *It might look like junk now, but Ma had loved it all.*

Her Ma used to say you could judge a person by what you couldn't always see — the way they kept their drawers and cupboards, for example. Ma's kitchen cupboards had always been neat as a pin — all those Campbell soup cans lined up on the shelves so you could read the labels, her homemade jams and jellies organized by contents and date. Or the state of their underwear...

"That Dorothy Jenkins is a slob," Ma announced during some long-ago lunch. "I know for a fact she never folds her underwear and only stuffs it into the drawer."

"What difference does it make?" Donna was rewarded with one of her mother's piercing glares.

"Any decent woman folds her undies and puts them away tidy." Her mother tilted her chin defiantly and looked out the kitchen window.

"And how do you know 'for a fact' anyway? Were you snooping in her drawers?"

Gasping, Ma turned her eyes slowly back from the window, and said, "Don't you get smart mouthed with me now." Donna didn't need an answer, the sudden flush to Ma's face said it all.

Donna was shocked when she started going through her mother's house after the funeral. How long had it been since she had gone upstairs? Must have been years, judging by the state of things.

"Gonna need a dumpster," Ralph said as he followed her through the second floor hallway. Donna had sagged onto her mother's bed and put her head in her hands as her husband ticked off all the things that were "just plain not worth saving."

The next day, though, she rallied to the task. Arranging for the dumpster was a cinch. The man at Mid-State Haulers must have sensed her embarrassment. "We do it all the time," he said on the phone. "If folks didn't hold onto all that stuff, I'd be out of business like that!" She heard the snap of his fingers.

Once the dumpster was parked in the side yard, it was pretty easy to get rid of the useless stuff. For three weeks she had sifted mindlessly through thirty years — *thirty?* — of junk mail, *Redbooks* and *Good Housekeepings*, torn clothing and old shoes. It turned out the dumpster wasn't too big, after all.

By the end of that first month, she and Ralph had thrown out every worthless thing. The house was stripped to its bare walls — drawers and closets empty, linens and furniture cleaned for the yard sale. She scrubbed floors, sanitized the old kitchen and bathroom, washed windows and woodwork.

Sunlight bounced through the now-curtainless windows into rooms that had been kept in semi-darkness for years. It no longer felt like her mother's home. It was just some old farmhouse waiting to be sold.

She had cleaned out her mother's room first, so she could sleep in there. When she opened one dresser, she cried out in surprise. Her Ma's underwear was packed so tightly into the little drawer that Donna had to yank hard to open it. When it came free, the faint aromas of Ivory soap, rosewater, and other scents that had always lingered over Ma wafted up. As she dumped the contents of the little drawer on the bed, she saw that each panty had been carefully folded. *Why did she need so many?*

Every night, Donna would fall into bed, exhausted. She had found her mother's last book — *another damn romance.* As she sat on the edge of the bed, book in hand, a receipt from Parker's Store holding her mother's place, Donna felt a brief pang. She pictured Ma lying in bed at night under the glow of the old, pink reading lamp that hung from the mahogany headboard. *She never finished the story*, she thought as she closed the book and returned it to the table, next to her mother's reading glasses.

Most nights, Donna would prop up the pillows and read for a half hour before turning out the light. On the third night, she opened the novel and began to read. As she pored over the pages — *an easy read* — she found herself reconnecting with her mother. She paused, laid the book aside and drifted back to her high school days.

How many dates had she come home from, to find her mother propped in bed just like this, reading glasses sliding down her nose, ready to listen to whatever Donna had to say? Oh, the conversations they'd had. Donna told her mother everything, and Ma never judged or chastised her — only listened, occasionally giving some subtly disguised advice.

"You were always there, Ma," Donna whispered to the shadowed corners of the room. "I wish you were here now so I could talk to you one more time." And then, she began to talk to her mother as she hadn't for years. She told her about the unfulfilled dream of going cross-country with Ralph, of how they had always said they'd do it "next year" or "when we can save up." It was then that she thought she heard her mother say, "Do it now, hon. Take the money from the house and do it now before it's too late."

She jerked awake, saying, "Huh?" but there was no answer. Her mother had faded into the shadows again. As she pulled the reading lamp's chain, she whispered into the dark, "I'll do it, Ma. This time I will."

Five weeks to the day after the funeral, she walked into the *Weekly Sentinel* office, ready to take out an ad for the yard sale. Maryanne Sloane had been sitting at the receptionist's desk for so many years that Donna couldn't remember who had been there before.

"So sorry for your troubles, Donna," Maryanne offered her version of standard local sympathies. "Your mother was a good woman. Sad that she had to die all alone like that."

Going through the ritual was more annoying than comforting for Donna, so she plunged right ahead into the business at hand. She placed the ad, bought yellow "Yard Sale" signs for both ends of the street, and was out the door in ten minutes flat.

"*Excuse* me." It was the lady with the mug again. "I asked how much for that old lamp over there."

"It's not for sale."

She didn't like the way the woman bickered over everything, making Donna feel like a cheapskate, when it was the woman who was being stingy. She didn't want her to have any of her mother's things.

"Hey, this is a yard sale and that lamp is out on the lawn. If it's out here, it's for sale." The lady's face reddened.

"No, it's not," Donna said. "It's out here because I'm going to get it re-paired." *What! Donna didn't want the old thing.*

"I'll give you *one hundred* dollars for it," the woman said.

"It's *NOT* for sale." Donna turned away and began gathering things up to take inside.

The woman put her hand on Donna's shoulder and shoved. "One fifty, and not a penny more!"

"Don't push me, ma'am. It is not for sale. I'm keeping it."

Sweat gleamed on the woman's upper lip. She swiped at it with her hand.

"Three hundred. We **both** know it's not worth more than that." She fumbled in her big straw bag, pulling out a wad of bills. With shaking hands she peeled off twenties and tens and tried to thrust them at Donna.

Donna was stunned, both by the woman's outrage and by the amount of money she was offering for the lamp. Had it been in their lives so long that they failed to see its value? Or was its value to them only in the light it shed on their reading? Ma had always leaned towards romance novels, while Donna preferred mysteries and anything by Robert Ludlum.

For a moment, she was flustered, giving the woman enough time to put the crumpled bills in Donna's hand and stride off with the lamp. Donna watched in disbelief as she put it in the back of her station wagon and slammed the hatch. As she backed out, Donna shouted, "Hey! You didn't pay for the mug." The woman flipped her middle finger as she drove off.

Donna smoothed the bills out and put them in the blue Maxwell House can with the rest of the morning's proceeds. Tucking the can under her right arm, she picked up the box of moldy paperbacks and headed for the barn.

Inside its cool darkness, she put the box on the worn floor, and sat on it. Looking at the bills stuffed into the coffee can, she thought *Is this what it all comes down to? A warm May morning, and a can of money? Is this what you spent all those years pack ratting for, Ma? So I could have a can of money?*

How Much?

She didn't think so, but she wasn't sure. Her mother had always wanted her to be free — no worries, no cares. She had admired Donna's spirited lifestyle. "If I was 20 years younger, I'd go with you," she used to say whenever Donna headed out in her old VW bus. Her mother was saddened more by Donna's settling down with Ralph and giving up her free-wheeling life than Donna ever had been.

How many times had Ma asked "Are you happy, *really* happy?"

When she stood to go outside again, she had a sudden flash. She saw herself 40-odd years ago in this very barn. Her father was pushing her on the swing that hung from the loft.

They had been singing some silly song as he pushed her higher and higher. Donna could almost feel the rough rope, and the swing's worn, wooden seat. On the final push — just at its apex — she had jumped. "Donna!" Dad shouted, "No!"

Out the open door she had sailed, her head narrowly missing the doorframe. Into the sunlight, feet first, she felt like she flew on for hours. The arc of her flight brought her almost to the rosebush. She landed on her feet, her red Keds skidding in the dewy grass, and she crashed into the thorny *Rugosa*.

Donna laughed at the memory of her father running to lift her out of the big bush. "Donna! What were you thinking?" he asked brushing imaginary dirt from her dress. She had seen tears in his eyes before he pulled her tight to his chest, and she could still hear the loud thumping of his heart — the same heart that would fail him not ten years later.

"I can fly, Dad! I can fly!" she had whispered into the soft, blue fabric of his shirt.

"Yes, you can," he had whispered back.

As she worked lugging the odds and ends back in the barn, Donna thought about how things would be when the house was sold, and she could walk out of it for good. Maybe if we're careful with the money, we could head out west, she thought. She wondered just how much they'd have when all was said and done.

Hell, she thought, *Ralph's never been across the country.* Since Ma died, they had talked about just up and going. Each conversation ended with Ralph saying, "I don't know, Donna. We aren't getting any younger. We might just want to hold onto what we get."

She thought of her Dad, dead all these years, and Ma, so recently gone. They always had faith in her. She was their shining hope — the one buzzing, swirling star in the constellation of their dreams.

"All we ever want for you, Donna, is that you always have enough to get by," her Dad said when she graduated from high school, "and that you follow your dreams.

"Dreams are important," he continued. "Don't you ever let anybody talk you out of them." Her parents' gift to her had been the VW bus; she had climbed aboard three days after graduation and set off for her first adventure — a month-long trip to the Rockies that stretched into two years on the road.

As she paused in the barn door to wipe sweat from her brow, a red Chevy pickup drove in, gears grinding as it lurched to a stop. *Must be a '51 or '52* she thought as the driver threw open the door and jumped out.

"Am I too late?" he asked. "I drove by earlier, but I couldn't stop, and then the next thing I knew it was after twelve," he looked around the yard. "Not much left, eh?"

"There's stuff in the barn," she gestured over her shoulder. "What year's your truck — '51?" Just then she saw the *For Sale* sign in the rear window. "You're selling that truck?"

Donna walked over and rubbed the shiny curve of the front fender.

"She'a a beaut, ain't she? " he grinned, shoving his baseball cap back to scratch the top of his head. "Belonged to my brother. I tell ya, he sure loved that old truck. It's a '52, by the way.

"Get behind the wheel and see how good it feels," he said as he opened the driver's door. "Totally restored, right down to the distributor cap. Old Johnny was a fiend for gettin' everything just so. 'Course the paint's not original, but he just had to paint her candy apple red. Whaddya think? Damn fine, ain't she?"

He sure talks a lot. "Damn fine," she agreed, resting her hands on the wheel. "How much do you want?"

When he told her the price, she did a quick calculation. Even before selling the house, she knew they could buy it. He kept talking, something about need-ing the money and not really loving the truck like his brother had, but Donna wasn't paying attention. She saw them — Ralph and her — riding in the red Chevy, saw the road stretching out before them — farmlands and prairie, small towns and mountains — all the way to the west coast. She saw big, open sky, stars that went on forever over their heads.

"*How* much?" she asked again, but it really didn't matter. ∎

Maureen Farr

Midnight Lunch

My mother visits at odd hours.
Not like before,
when she arrived,
sat on the edge of her seat,
foot tapping,
coat shrugged open.

Now, she comes at 3 a.m.
dressed for lunch.

We go to places
we've never been,
and I'm sure she
wouldn't dream of.

She eats
food she never
ordered in her life.

Like this morning, 4:15.
We go to lunch and order
Etruscan chicken for her,
a hamburger for me.

She, who never liked chicken,
orders —no, craves it —
and eats with gusto.

Why not? This is my dream.
For once in my life
she does what I want.
Rome, April 9, 2006
(from the dream poems)

Hendrik D. Gideonse

An Electric Blanket Gone South

We lie within the chilly bed,
Your breasts molded to my back,
Unmistakable,
Though two layers of flannel intercede;
The tops of your thighs
Lightly frost the bottoms of mine.
The inside of your left calf
Edges over the outside left of mine.
I feel your cool sole slide and
Touch my metatarsals.

And then the bedclothes lose their chill.
The rise is slow,
Almost imperceptible,
Until one moment just past the next
The cold is neutralized and gone.

Comfort creeps upon us, as
Slowly, hearth and home are built,
Or children grow and go,
Or careers reach their peak and then,
Like gums, slightly recede.
The years together add stealth
And luscious patience to the repertoire.

We stir;
The comfort zone expands.
Warmth's slow contagion makes us turn
To nuzzle, kiss, caress,
And dance the dance four hundred months
Have given us time to hone.

Hendrik D. Gideonse

Picture in a Restaurant Window

They first came into view in mirrored glass
As by Dmitri's window they passed
From left to right, she, pretty, slight,
Round face, bubbling, her chest tight
To his broad back, hands flicking at his sides,
Though something said they'd rather play his thighs.

The two pass from view; I maintain my gaze,
And then an older woman takes their place,
Comfortable of build, seventy, I'd say,
She's made her Peter-Pan-collared way
From right to left, her gaze thrown to the rear
On the pair whose besotment was that clear.

She slowed her walk, turned more tightly
In her stare, but soon it softened; she lightly
Grinned, which then spilled wide,
As if to say she's satisfied
Her memories – and mine – grant clemency,
Two pardoned eavesdrops, not heard but seen,
As we both rode, in layered self-reflection,
Small thermals of remembered affection.

Hendrik D. Gideonse

Hands

Her face first touched me in the opera door,
Actually not her face at all — that came later —
Just the side of her cheek, and abundant, framing, leonine hair.
I couldn't see her eyes or brow or lips;
I couldn't even catch a smile
If, in fact, she wore one, but something about
Her posture said care, intent, intensity.
By God, she really caught my eye!

I let the moment pass.

I showed my ticket; the taker waved me by.
I found my friends and took not my usual seat on an aisle
To serve my legs but one seat over
To be flanked by my female friends. And Tim?
Well, he could just take the fourth seat in.
I turned left to him to talk
And caught my second glimpse of her,
Sliding in the very row the four of us had found.
I noticed — but didn't, you know,
Reserve and sense of subtlety being what they are.

I'm still turned to speak with Tim,
And she leans out to speak with the person to her right.
We catch each other's glance, wide-eyed,
Full on, face to face, twelve feet apart.
I struggle, unobtrusively, I hope, to keep my cool,
A single moment, frozen in my time.

One of us turned away first — I can't remember who.
I leaned back against the seat
Just head and eyes turned left.
I saw her forearm and her hand —
Gesturing,
Smoothing the program,
Resting on her thigh,
A thin hand, dark, I think, or, rather, tanned,
Tendons lightly raised fan-like on the back,
A gentle hand yet firm,
A hand that — odd thought — seemed somehow full of hope.

The performance closed.
I'd actually taken out a card to introduce myself,
An act so bold, so off my norm,
It quite filled me with surprise.
I hung back.
My party climbed the aisle.
I had her in my sight,
And then found her gone,
And then once more in view
Talking earnestly to a young man I knew.
Not daring to stare, I lost sight once more,
But he'd not left,
So I asked him who the woman was
On whom his attention centered.
He answered.
I grinned, felt foolish, turned red.
"Oh, that's my mom," he'd said.

MLK, Jr
May 6, 1964
First Parish Church, Brunswick, ME

Among the twelve hundred attending
There was at first silence,
Expectation, admiration,
A collective holding of breath.

The Baptist hero standing
An arm's length away
In this Congregational pulpit
Was recognizable even from behind,
His shoulders braced,
Head tilted up,
The surfaces of his robe beginning to whisper
As his body moved in time.

Rhythmical, resonant,
His voice complemented the deep mahogany tones
Of the polished lectern
Standing free of text or notes.

This pulpit had heard
Songs of intellect over time –
Jane Addams, Harriet Beecher Stowe,
Henry Wadsworth Longfellow,
Ralph Waldo Emerson, Henry Ward Beecher,
Eleanor Roosevelt –
And all the time that Martin spoke
His hands and fingers ranged –
They an even darker hue than the wood itself –

Taking readings of the molding,
The lectern's surfaces,
The pulpit rail,
Transcendent caresses
Running up and down the fluted edges
Drawing energy and inspiration
From wood oiled by the essence
Of twelve decades of principled ferment,
Each touch summoning precious harmonies
To the deeply moral civil symphony
Issuing from his lips.

Hendrik D. Gideonse

Tendrils

The stairway to the second floor was tight;
Despite the open spindles on its side,
It always felt a narrow passage.
Its steep treads ended in a landing;
One stepped up to the right and doubled back
To gain access to the rest of the house.
But you couldn't climb those stairs without passing
The fair-sized room over the two-car garage
Lying, also up a step, at the stairway's head.

This was my father's study.

Bookshelves lined the walls from floor to ceiling
Save only for window spaces on three sides and
The closet door. The narrow space behind that door
Housed a four-drawer file,
A tidal flow of Barricini chocolates
In their many bags and boxes,
And, for several years, his mother's ashes
Until *my* mother, with planning, ceremony
And deliberate choice of place,
Dumped the old Tartar's remains in Gibraltar's strait!
My father's parakeets and Java birds hung out there;
Sometimes they flew free and tongued his
Cheeks and spectacles for salt —
"Pood-chee, pood-chee" he'd intone to bring them near.

When he was in this space the music flowed —
Beethoven, Sousa, Strauss, and Bach,
Rodgers, Gershwin, Lowe, Dvorak.
Two wingback chairs hunkered heavy there.
Under and on the large table I'd built for him

Sprouted unkempt paper stacks,
But to he who'd grown them,
They were finely calibrated sets
Of archeologically defined — and precisely recalled — strata.
In this room as a brand-new teen I first found and
Shared with younger brother, Marty,
The three fat folios of photographic nudes,
Visual preparation with great aesthetic style
For corporeal adventures we each would have in years ahead.

A two-tiered table lamp held ashtrays, pencil jars and clips,
Spring-loaded shears for slicing out the news,
And a penknife.
On every vacant space and edge stood objets d'art,
Mementos of his travels round the globe.
This room was where my father spent
The greatest portion of his day when he was home;
He'd read, and annotate, and write text
On small white pads with #2 pencils always needing to be sharpened,
The penknife being the only tool I ever saw him use.
His script, if that not be dignifying it too much,
Only his secretary and, sometimes, my mother could decode.
Phillip Morris English Ovals resided here,
The slightly oblong boxes pleasing to the eye and hand,
A triumph of design,
The lidded top mating perfect to the base,
The folded over inner parchment wrap
Needing to be spread to reach the smokes inside.
He'd often forget he'd have one lit lying steady in his hand,
With its ever longer Cat-in-the-Stovepipe-Hat ash,
Smoke slowly curling by his index and middle fingers,
The tendril plume flowing straight up in the air
And then abruptly falling on itself like ribbon candy,
Forgotten streams of smoke
That dyed those left hand fingers a burnished gold.
Music foretold his presence when in residence.
And just in case your ears were numb or otherwise engaged,
The swirling, lazy trails of exhaled smoke
Or just the pungent smell proclaimed him there.
This was his Sanctum Sanctorum wherein did dwell
The mighty power,

Hendrik D. Gideonse

Mysterious,
Dark,
Ominous,
Portending hell
(Or so it seemed).
The wing chairs cradled the lanky, solid frame
Whose life force smoldered for ideas and words,
And the worlds those words defined,
Or shook,
Or split,
Or built,
Or canted ever slightly out of whack …
Or blew to smithereens.

We rarely entered when he was home,
As much because we knew he mustn't be disturbed —
Or certainly we dared not —
As because there wasn't much with him we felt we shared
Save for the music, birds, and once a week our trips
To pay a dollar on account against the balance of the latest loan
Although I do recall a dollar flowing once the other way
The day I showed I'd met his challenge to commit
The Gettysburg address to memory.

At arm's length, we were, it turns out, no less securely held.
We later — much later — learned, it was often for our good,
But sometimes staining, too,
For, unrecognized and seldom felt,
His clasp entangled every sector of our lives,
Like smoke spilling from his study door
Seeping under all the thresholds of the house,
Reaching every floor.

Waltzing with Bracey

This time of year, the wind rattles the bedroom windows, whistles through them, shakes the sashes. Slammed by northwesters all winter, knocked about like a ship at sea, my house shudders and quivers in tune with Wagnerian elemental forces. A steady bass roar of waves a hundred feet away in the bay is overlaid by staccato gusts hitting the corners of the house. On the western shore of Deer Isle, this drafty, old family summer "cottage," inherited from my aunt, faces a heart-stopping view of the Camden Hills twenty miles across Penobscot Bay.

It's early December. I decide to make more of a winter bed for Bracey, my Welsh corgi, and me in my uninsulated house. First, I lay a blanket on the bare mattress, a flannel sheet over it, then a bottom sheet, a top sheet, a second electric blanket, another blanket, and, finally, another flannel sheet so Bracey's hairs don't get over everything. With all these layers, the bed is like a club sandwich. At the foot is my new queen-size quilt, which I'll pull up a little at a time depending on the temperature. It'll probably end up over our heads before the night is through.

Bracey, who doesn't like the noise of wind in the bedroom at night, often retreats downstairs to his round, Black Watch L.L. Bean dog bed by the wood-stove in the kitchen. He feels safer at ground level, away from the wind's walloping upward thrusts.

Most of the time, he remains on my bed, sleeping restlessly with his ears back, eyelids and whiskers twitching. It's crowded with Bracey on this bed, but he doesn't notice. He stretches out on top of his flannel sheet alongside me the way he must have as a puppy with his mother. He makes a good hot water bottle. Whenever I turn over and draw up my knees, he switches around to put his head on my hip, his rear end hanging over the edge of the bed. He growls softly as my position shifts, but soon adjusts.

A few days ago, when it was my turn to host the Morning Deer Isle Writers Group, all the pipes in the house froze. It took me three hours to defrost them with a hair drier.

"It's thirty-five degrees in my kitchen!" I screamed to one of the writers on the phone at 6:00 A.M.

The only heat came from the woodstove. If I opened the cabinet doors, I was hit by drafts. I plugged cracks in the kitchen walls with fiberglass insulation. Bracey thought the spumy pink puffs were dog chewies.

I hung pale green quilted bedspreads in the doorways, draped red-plaid Hudson Bay blankets on the chairs, heaped hooked and braided rugs on the floor. The kitchen looked like an antique New England version of a Turkish tent.

"And what are you doing?" I said to Bracey as he stood, motionless, at his water bowl. Finally, I noticed the water was frozen.

"You poor baby." I poured boiling water on the ice. In no time it cooled enough for him to drink.

"I'm living an experiment," I told the writers when they arrived at 9:00 A.M.

I'd been an art books editor in New York City for thirty years, with little experience of rural existence. I was trying to decide whether I wanted to stay in this house year round, meet its challenges.

"Is it crazy to inhabit this big, blusterous house?" I asked the writers. Wrapped in blankets in my kitchen, feet on footstools, they still wore their wool hats and gloves.

"My nearest neighbor is a mile away! What if I trip over Bracey and break my leg?"

"Don't worry," Nancy said, raising the earflaps on her husband's Gore-Tex hat. "In a few years, you'll be complaining about the new houses next door." She lowered the flaps, pulled the Hudson Bay blanket up to her chin.

The writers placed their notebooks on their laps and tried to write, but it was too cold. Talking for a while longer, clouds of steam hovering around their mouths, they soon left.

After they'd gone, I talked to Bracey.

"This is my first real home — your first real home — the first I've owned," I said. "But we can always return to New York. I've made no decision yet."

Bracey, lying on a pile of rugs near the woodstove, appeared stoic and composed.

I talk to him a lot. I consult with him before I haul the wood or fetch the mail. I tell him about the opera we hear on the radio. He has listened all his life to the Saturday afternoon Metropolitan Opera broadcasts and has acquired an appreciation of music. He expects such conversations, wants to know these things, pays full attention.

In our new life here, no matter what the temperature or season, Bracey and I have an evening ritual. Before we climb upstairs, we go outside for our bedtime walk. Unless it's raining — the only weather he dislikes, especially thunder and lightning — we circumnavigate the house slowly while he sniffs to see what creatures have been in the long grass and under the trees and along the driveway — his gossip column, his salt air society.

He will not be rushed in his pursuit of every last delicious tidbit. Occasionally, he halts in his tracks, ears pointed forward toward the blackness, a low growl in his throat. I beam my flashlight into the dark recesses of the woods, imagining murderers, assassins, but he continues his leisurely way, taking a whiff of dead iris and hosta, detouring to a patch of blackened monk's hood for a quick pee, absorbed, concentrated, a pro on the job.

Halfway in our circuit, we stop at the wooden bench on the point where there's a 180-degree view of the bay and the islands. Sometimes the moonlit view is as clear as in daylight, the islands low on the curved horizon, the water a silvery globe. Other times it's an impenetrable black and only the sound of the surf signals the ocean's presence. I back off from this darkness, threatened by the cold sound of the waves, by the unseen expanse, longing for New York and the bright, crowded streets of the Upper West Side.

We're safer on this point, however, than we were among the drug dealers and hangers-on who used to congregate outside my apartment building on the east side of Amsterdam Avenue at 93rd Street. An armed guard finally was hired to patrol our block, so the drug dealers, whom Bracey and I recognized and who recognized us from our frequent walks, simply moved to the west side of the avenue.

Bracey doesn't seem to miss New York. Perhaps he's forgotten the satisfaction he derived from smelling the trees growing in patches of dirt on the sidewalks of our neighborhood or from running into the poodles, Labs, and goldens he used to see on the streets every day.

He also tried herding — his true occupation — dogs in Central Park until they turned on him and snapped. In the North Meadow one time, deluded into thinking he was consequential and had a duty to perform, and that nothing must divert him from his task, he barked louder and louder, the better to do the job. Hush! cried the dog owners, but he couldn't stop himself. Only after all the dogs, followed by their mistresses and masters, had fled to Central Park West, back to their apartment buildings, did he look around and see what he had done. His officiousness had driven them away.

Bracey and I used to walk around the Central Park Reservoir every morning. I was always on the lookout for a friend for Bracey or a playgroup that wouldn't treat him like an outsider. I remember a clear fall day, when Bracey was still a puppy, an Afghan appeared on the brow of a hill to the north of the reservoir. The west wind ruffled his silky hair, teased his delicate, long topknot. Outlined against the early morning sky, Heathcliff on Dartmoor, he stared intently into the distance.

"Here's a pal for you," I told Bracey. "He's big, but he appears to be thoughtful, sensitive. Anyway, you like them big."

Bracey and I climbed the hill. Still focused elsewhere, the Afghan ignored us. We headed toward him. Over the rise, in a delicious, small hollow surrounded by great oaks and maples, a dozen dogs—beardless collies, shelties, Jack Russells, mutts — roughhoused, hurled themselves at one another, and ran for balls and Frisbees, mad with the joy of sociability. I couldn't believe our luck.

A clump of people stood at one end of the hollow, facing the dogs. I felt shy. For Bracey's sake, I had to make the effort.

We descended into the vale, Bracey, at first, like me, hanging back. The playing field was a muddy pit, a cauldron of furry legs and paws, snapping jaws. Leaves were everywhere, tossed into the air like snowflakes in a February blizzard. Bracey looked at me.

"Go in there," I said. He headed into the maelstrom, crouching as low as he could, nose to the ground.

What did these seasoned, sophisticated New Yorkers in their Adidas, wide-shouldered parkas, and becoming fedoras talk about, I wondered, forgetting I might be considered one of them by some.

I sidled up, hung on the fringe. No one turned around.

"She won't eat her Iams minichunks. She scatters them on the kitchen floor," a young man with shaved head and woven aqua scarf said.

"Sascha didn't eat his minichunks for five days. Give her time," said a woman in a lilac jacket.

"Sheba shredded the Saturday *Times* last night. My mother was over for dinner. She was hysterical. 'Is this the way you're bringing her up?' she asked me," said a heavyset man in a business suit.

"Look, there's a corgi! A beautiful corgi! Where'd he come from?" Spinning and pirouetting, Bracey was smack in the center of the galvanic storm of barks, woofs, snarls.

"He's mine!" I said, ready to be witty, informative, anything they wished.

"He's gorgeous." "How old is he?" "What's his name?" "Where'd you get him?" they asked, still with their backs to me.

I watched the dogs surround Bracey, sniff him, cuff him. Delirious with happiness, his long muzzle opened wide with passionate, jubilant barking, he was Otello crying "Esultate" after his victory over the Turks. King of the moment, he was the newest — and the handsomest — guy on the block.

"Six months," I said. "His name's Bracey."

"He's a baby, a love! How much does he weigh?"

After this encounter, on our daily two-mile circuit of the reservoir, along with swarms of joggers and walkers, people said hello to Bracey by name, and asked him how he was.

He swaggered a bit, his fetching, tail-less bottom waggling in three-quarter time. Made me proud.

In Maine, he doesn't have this kind of recognition. But he loves his walks here. Willing to take risks, pad into the unknown, he's an adventurer.

At night, when the full moon hangs over Eagle Island to the south, Bracey walks through shadows cast on the frozen ground by spruces along the shore. The shadows look like animals to me. Ambling across a camel, Bracey stops to snuffle the dried stalks of delphinium, blurring the crisp outline of the dromedary's face.

Animals lie all around the house in the winter moonlight. Bracey and I have to watch our step. They are far bigger than Bracey. In fact, they consume him.

He makes his way to a bison, its shaggy, heavy chest dragging the snow-packed earth, then to a fat rabbit with large ears sitting sideways beside phantom, coal-black hollyhocks, sweet peas, and ferns profiled in the snow. As we walk south, the moon sinks behind the trees, the shadows lengthen and deepen, and I almost stumble where the terrain suddenly darkens.

I look down, straight into nothingness. Bracey disappears, head first. I hear him mushing in the blackness, see movement among illusory daisies. We are near the water.

I panic and call him.

"Bracey, where are you? Come out! Quick!"

Could he have fallen over the bank? I can't see him in the drift of snow.

I begin to discern images of emerging trees, as in a photographer's developing tray. More details issue, little by little: slender, two-inch spruce cones and long, slightly curved needles.

Finally, I see Bracey. He walks where I fear to. He saunters over a snow goose, steps on its large black wingtips.

"Careful, Bracey!"

In unknown territory — jungle, Lascaux cave, primeval forest — we are surrounded. I want to return to the house, put on a CD of *Der Fliegende Holländer*, stoke the woodstove, draw a hot bath, get into my flannel pajamas, my warm sheets, cover my head with blankets. Bracey is back with the rabbit, which has shifted its position, now facing me. I pat the rabbit's head, reach into its eyes to touch Bracey, feel a furry chest against my hand.

From the kitchen window the next morning, the sea looks closer, brought deceptively nearer by the new snow that fell in the night. All traces of our walk hours before are gone. The twisted trunks of spruces silhouetted against the water are black, the tall rust-colored grass under them a golden glow, the rugosa a shocking splash of yellow in the coldness. I let Bracey out into this scene.

It's a winter palette, a winter Winslow Homer palette, authenticated by Bracey in his fox-red coat wriggling on his back, making corgi angels in the snow.

Bracey's thick coat keeps him warm. He's not aware that we're living in a cold house under arctic conditions. His position inside the sunny back door, from which he surveys his exterior world of crows, gulls, and squirrels, is secure. But Islanders are taking bets how long we can last.

In mid-December, I ask a carpenter friend, Gary, to insulate part of my house, to form a warm space for Bracey and me, a house-within-a-house. Built in 1902, the shingle building has an open L-shaped plan, with a large living room, kitchen, and pantry, and five bedrooms upstairs. It was designed by Alexander Wadsworth Longfellow, the poet's nephew, for another uncle of his, my great-uncle James Greenleaf Croswell.

In awe of my own house, I'm reluctant to change a thing. In its presence, I feel like a little girl, rather than an aging, single, slightly eccentric woman who has taken up writing in her isolated, hip-roofed "cottage."

Perhaps if I start small…

I decide to begin with my bedroom, study, and bathroom. Gary frames in the outside walls and inserts three-and-a-half-inch fiberglass batting; then tapes and muds. Tess, his wife, paints the bathroom pale blue with dark blue splashes: the wall behind the tub, the slanted beam, and the antique, wooden water tank six feet overhead from which the toilet is flushed with a chain.

Roman, their large, gentle dog, part wolf, accompanies them to work. Bracey and Roman play among the rolls of fiberglass and coils of tape. I worry at first: a wolf amusing himself with my corgi?

"He's a living doll," Gary says. "I bought him from a guy who breeds them. Swore he wouldn't hurt a baby."

Gary's on a ladder in the tiny study, plastering the ceiling overhead, his long brown hair spattered with white pulp. Through the dormer window, I see Roman bounding and leaping in the snow with Bracey. He looks back at Bracey to see if he's close behind, slowing down to let him catch up.

"He's a gentleman," I say.

Then he flattens his lanky torso on the snow and Bracey goes nose-to-nose with him.

"I think Bracey's in love with Roman," I say.

"And with you, too, Gary," I add.

When Gary arrives at the house each morning, he sits on the floor and plays with Bracey. Cradling him in his arms, he invites kisses. An expression of rapture — brown eyes half-closed in enchantment, black nostrils shining — spreads over Bracey's face.

It's becoming habitable upstairs. The heat from the woodstove in the kitchen rises through a register to warm my bedroom. I begin to dream of building a small, insulated addition, of making this end a year-round house. I'm learning to be brave, like Bracey. I consult friends: Can Bracey and I survive on my isolated point? Can I build onto my family house? Live with my ghosts? Tamper with Longfellow's original design?

At a party toward the end of December, I meet Don, an architect, who says, "Do the drawings yourself. I'll critique them."

Using an engineer's ruler and furniture templates, I make drawings on graph paper. Braccy remains calm, but curious, as I crawl on the floor to do my measurements. He supposes I'm down there to play.

In a frenzy of dreaming, I sketch dozens of plans and variations. I glass in the small screen porch facing west to the water, extend six feet on the southeastern side toward the sun, add on nine feet to the north. I take my portfolio of drawings to Don.

He discards all but a drawing of the addition to the north. Using a heavy pencil on tracing paper, he widens and expands it.

"But …" I say.

And it's done. The first of Don's many divine drawings of my addition.

"The floors will be warmer," I tell Bracey on our way home. "We will have new yellow pine floors."

We have to wait until May — until the snow melts and the ground is soft — before Gary returns.

Gary slices lumber with screeching machines. Music to his ears, Bracey observes unflinchingly. He witnesses posts poured, old bead board stripped, and walls pushed out. He's vigilant as two-by-four studs and floor and ceiling joists are installed; he patrols the perimeter as cedar shingles are nailed. He listens to Don and Gary talk about soffits and fascias and flashing. With Gary and Roman back, life is good. Bracey follows them everywhere.

I invite the plumbers, electricians, painters, and cabinet-makers to bring their dogs to work. Carol has her mutt and a golden; Jay, her poodle mix; Tony, his hound. It's dog heaven. One day there are seven dogs.

Bracey reigns supreme. But once in a while, he goes too far and tries to herd his friends, forgetting what happened in Central Park. The dogs don't run off this time, but remain planted in the Maine earth, snarling at his oafishness.

"It's a trade-off, Bracey," I tell him "Either you keep them as pals or treat them like cattle."

I must deal with my choices, as well, although of a different order.

"Do you want fine cherry-wood edging on the cabinet tops?" asks Don, offering Bracey a biscuit. "Do you think three electric outlets next to the kitchen peninsula are sufficient? Four at the foot of the stairs?" asks Sonny, the electrician, stroking Bracey's tummy with his powerhouse hands. "Do you wish to keep the old toilet in the upstairs bathroom?" asks Tony, the plumber, patting Bracey on his rear.

These questions send me into a frenzy of uncertainty.

But slowly, my fixers, Don and the builders of my dream, create a magic box where I can live in beauty and solitude. The sea fills the big glass windowpanes to the brim, lighting the white walls, the yellow pine floors, the whole room awash in reflected sea light, a creamy blue aquarium of riches.

Bracey enjoys the expansiveness of floor, the sun on the soft, nubby rug. He sets aside his herding failures and delights in the company of dogs.

I grow in confidence, too, thriving on the new growing out of the old like a flower blossoming on an old woody stem. I learn to sing back to my family ghosts: I'm composing an enchanted life in my room awash in sea grays and music greens.

Gary concludes his part of the job. Tying up loose ends is not his style.

Jorge, another master carpenter, finishes the details. Jorge is a perfectionist, an archangel, a miracle-maker, who wears a John-the-Baptist beard and speaks in a gentle, Spanish-accented voice.

If I mention a leak of cold air in the bedroom floor over the porch, he goes at the matter with the tenaciousness of a longhaired dachshund after a mole. He tracks down small and large leaks, subtle whiffs and prolonged breezes, putting his cheeks to the floorboards, Bracey behind him sniffing in his wake. He uses cans of foam, silicone tubes, caulking guns, climbing on tall ladders to apply glues — puffy, spreading gels, gums, and clear liquids — to the cracks and holes above windows, around doors, behind shelves. Bracey is in ecstasy, poking his nose in the cans and tubes.

I make lists of my own discoveries of these tiny cracks, slits in my citadel, as fifty mile-an-hour winds send chilly arrows across my ankles and shoulders.

Bracey worships Jorge, this man who works with tools, this bearded fellow, this Old Testament visionary. Head on paws, totally absorbed, his eyes follow Jorge's quiet, meticulous hands as they lift the treasures, the planes and saws and bits, from their archive, his fabulous tool-chest of instruments, which, by his gifted labor, he makes sing.

Bracey listens, rapt, making a connection, perhaps, with other music he loves. When I tie my shoes in the front hall, he bursts forth in a full bass baritone as a prelude to our walk. He sounds much like Tito Gobbi or Bryn Terfel. Just yesterday, his bottom register had a beautiful sheen, like a clarinet.

We also dance, although with his short legs, dancing is not his forte.

Waltzing with Bracey

I danced with Bracey in our small New York apartment when he was a baby. One day, working at my desk editing a catalogue of the Peggy Guggenheim Collection, I heard Musetta's Waltz from *La Bohème* on the radio. I'd been telling Bracey how I'd waltzed as a child on skates in Switzerland, and as a girl in long, white tulle dresses at balls in the Plaza Hotel in New York. I was a debutante, I told him. Sometimes I'd take four boys in tuxedos with me to a dinner party and then on to a dance.

"Why Bracey, I'll teach you to waltz!"

Bracey was in his bed under my desk. He didn't move. In circuses, wearing clown hats and tutus, corgis jump through hoops and do tumbling acts, but waltz?

I dragged him out and held him upright by his forepaws. His back legs gave out. I picked him up and whirled him around the living room, bedroom, and kitchen to Musetta's Waltz until I was dizzy. He seemed to like the rhythm, the one-two-three beat. He certainly appreciated being held tight.

We danced to the "Blue Danube Waltz" and the waltzes in the *Nutcracker*. I could never resist the ones in *Der Rosenkavalier*. Once, when Kurt Moll as the drunken Baron Ochs sang the waltzes at the end of Act II, I sat on the floor, sobbing and mewling about how gorgeous and perfect the music was, and Bracey lay down beside me, patiently waiting for my operatic flood to subside.

In our house by the sea, Bracey and I still waltz. In fact, each time there's a waltz on the radio, Bracey comes to me and — I know this may sound silly — asks me to dance. ■

"Waltzing with Bracey" is an excerpt from the author's forthcoming memoir.

Cove Rhythms

A cormorant claims the jutting rock, black wings akimbo.
Sun worshipper, facing the open ocean.
Pterodactyl, guarding the channel entrance.

A man in a green canoe nods in obeisance,
glides silently by.
He hauls one over-wintered trap, throws the detritus
back into the black, forgiving water.

My dog whines at the door to the porch.
Two dead crabs lie at my feet, an offering.
Later, he calls attention to the kitchen door.
More crabs decorate the mat.

Max, I say, why these gifts from the sea?
We walk down to the shore.
More crabs float on the in-coming tide.
Max barks in delight, wags his tail.

The tide recedes; the clammer in the white truck
parks beside the woodpile,
arms himself with rake and rollers,
challenges the newly exposed mud.

Gayle Ashburn Hadley

Dog Days of Winter

In his maturity, the snow excites him.
He bounds outward, raised tail a plumy banner,
joyous barks sending crows aloft.

He attacks the nearest snowdrift, forepaws
working furiously to tunnel
into its cold mysterious depths.
Grabbing great mouthfuls of white fluff,
he spews them out again.

Interest in digging fades; chasing an imaginary prey,
he races five times around the yard perimeter,
spies a patch of ice.

He throws his shoulder and head down on the ice,
twists slightly, raises his haunches,
pumps furiously with hind legs,
propels himself across the shiny slickness.

This game, too, tires. He flops down on his back,
madly wriggles his torso in the snow,
makes doggie angels,
all four legs pawing the crisp air.

At last, exhausted, Max peers through the glass
of my kitchen door, whines,
"I'm ready for my nap. Let me in."

Family Reunion

Guillermo is polishing my bones. He's a good boy, taking his time and doing a thorough job. Respectful. Maria Teresa has brought him up right, even if she did have to do it by herself. That no-good she married – pah! I tried to warn her, but you know young women can't resist a pretty face. That Juan *was* good looking, even I admit that. But shallow, no staying power, weak, a flatterer. Soon enough he was drowning in tequila and she had to kick him out. Well, she's better off without him.

She's still my favorite granddaughter, and still beautiful, my Maria. Oh yes. Plenty of men still sniffing around her; none of them good enough. At least she knows this now. Oh, she has a little enjoyment now and then. Why not? I don't mind; things aren't like they used to be. Morals are looser today. Better maybe. Don't tell Sister Elena Francisca I said that. But I say, why shouldn't a woman have a good time now and then? Why should men have all the fun?

Guillermo is even better looking than his father; but so far he doesn't know that. It won't be long now, though, before he notices all those girls eyeing him, and discovers his power. Maria Theresa will have to chase them off with a broom.

She still follows the old ways; made a beautiful new handkerchief to hold my bones this coming year. She has embroidered it with my favorite flowers and a picture of Pepito. She didn't forget! How I loved that little dog. I was silly over him, I know. Sister Elena Francisca used to berate me for loving that dog so much. "Save such love for God, for Jesus, for the blessed Mother, for your family," she would scold. I didn't care. And her named after Santo Francisco, too. He knew how to love animals. Animals know when they are loved, just like people do. I bet Sister Elena never had a little enjoyment, shut up in that convent every night. Ha, Ha!

Listen to me, prattling on just like the old woman that I am. Or was.

Guillermo is sweating. He has had a lot to do out here in the hot sun. He started on the bones of his grandfather, my son-in-law, Jesus. His bones are in the top chamber; in the middle chamber are those of my daughter, Conchita. I'm in the bottom one. Yes, the mother-in-law is on the bottom. I suppose you think that's funny. Next to me, though, is my grandson, Tomas, Maria Teresa's brother. He was a sweet child. It nearly killed Conchita when he died, at age seven. The lung disease got him. So many of the children died young then, so many, so many. Too many tears to count. How did we survive, losing so many of our babies? All those hopes gone; our dreams dying with them.

I'm the last one in our tomb that the boy has to clean; Guillermo is almost finished. I can see that he is tempted to wipe his dripping forehead on the new cloth for my bones. He's a good boy, he resists. He wipes his sweat on the tail of his shirt instead.

Where is my husband, you ask? We didn't know where his bones were. That caused me such pain. Not to be able to bury him; to bring up his coffin after the three years and then to polish his bones; to have the two of us in this tomb. We should be in the top chamber together. Diego bought this tomb. We scrimped and saved for it. He, Diego, was the family patriarch, not my son-in-law. You see, Diego was carrying a load of lumber, driving in from the jungle in his truck. Both the lumber and the truck were valuable. We learned that the bandits got him. We never could find where they left his body. The men from our village searched for three days; Diego was well liked. The search was futile. The men came to my house, one or two at a time. They held their hats to their chests, hung their heads, not wanting to look directly in my face. They said their condolences in soft voices, some choking a little over the words.

Yes, living was hard. If only we had known what I know now, we would have felt differently about death. The living know so little, try as they might.

Tomorrow is a happy day for all our family, the living and the dead. Our annual family reunion: The Day of the Dead. Our bones will shine from the polishing. Next to our skulls, the many candles will glow softly as twilight nears. Maria Theresa and Guillermo will bring sweets shaped like skulls and little loaves of bread sprinkled with sugar. Maria makes this bread herself.

Did you know my neighbor, Frieda Gonzales? She is my neighbor in death as well as in life. Yes, she is in the next tomb over. And, you know what? Her family paid the cemetery worker, Jose Quintero, twenty-five pesos to clean her bones. They were too busy to take the time. And the little cakes, the sweets? Bought, all bought. Hah! ■

There's No Place Like Home

"The water in the bidet is hot," Ellie said. Then she giggled.

"Leave it to the French," Paul groused. He winced as he continued scraping his face using the lukewarm water at the bathroom sink. "This razor of yours is deadly. How can you stand to use it?"

Somehow, on the short flight from London to Paris, Paul's luggage had gone astray. Its delivery was promised for this afternoon.

"I still don't see why we couldn't have taken the chunnel," Paul said.

"I can't help it. The idea of that tunnel gives me the creeps. All that water on top of you, ugh! Then what happens if you meet up with a drunk driver? There's nowhere to go to get out of his way. Think of Princess Diana. I don't want to die like that."

Paul was coping, but having to wear yesterday's underwear, especially after sleeping in it, had put him in a foul mood. He was meticulous about his person.

"This is Paris, for God's sake. Do you know how these men look? I'm going in there with levis and a polo shirt. Talk about 'The Ugly American'."

"Honey, your presentation is fantastic. They won't be paying attention to your clothes."

"I doubt that. Say, what is your schedule today?" Paul asked.

"I'm meeting Jack and Susan for lunch. Susan has the afternoon booked at a fancy spa. When we talked last night, Jack said he might go to the Louvre with me."

The spa was very expensive. She felt envious of Jack and Susan, who were older and Jack was better established. Ellie had had to turn down Susan's offer to make an appointment for two.

"My meeting should last through most of the afternoon. Why don't you see if they want to meet for drinks and dinner? You can leave a message for me here at the hotel," Jack said.

"That sounds good. I might fit in a little shopping, too." This was a trial balloon.

Paul turned away from the mirror over the sink and regarded her with raised eyebrows.

"I can go window shopping at least," Ellie said. It had taken some persuasion for Paul to agree to bring her on this trip. They were supposed to be saving money to buy an apartment. That was to happen before they started a family. Paul always sounded so reasonable, so rational, when he talked about their plans. Ellie wasn't sure life was really supposed to be like that. She thought spontaneity was often a good thing; serendipity had its pleasures.

Ellie left the bathroom and returned to the bedroom. She poured herself another cup of coffee, added the hot milk, and put a second croissant on her plate. These were incredibly delicious, not at all like the ones at the corner bakery back home. She was reveling in the luxury of a good hotel, and better still, room service. Paul might have to rush out to his meeting, but she was on vacation. She was grateful her boss had let her take it now.

She thought of the day ahead with pleasure. Without Paul knowing, Ellie had bought herself a smart new outfit for this trip. It showed off her figure and matched the blue of her eyes. She would wear it today and surprise Paul at dinner.

Ellie thought about the possibility of spending the afternoon with Jack. She liked Jack. He was sophisticated but not intimidating. He knew how to talk to a woman and make her feel comfortable. Besides, he was very good looking. His hair was beginning to go gray at the temples, lending him a distinguished air. Yes, she would definitely wear the new outfit today.

Ellie spent a leisurely morning window shopping. She walked by shops with the names of Dior, Chanel. On the Avenue Marceau she gazed longingly in the window of Yves Saint Laurent. She was afraid to go in and try on any of the dresses because the clerks would surely know she couldn't afford one. In Galeries Lafayette, she bought a few gifts for relatives. She splurged on a silk necktie for Paul. Ellie thought it would be very smart to have a tie with a French label. Of course, the label wouldn't really show. Paul, raised in Manhattan, wouldn't care a fig, either, she realized. Guess I'll always be a farm girl, she admitted to herself. At least the tie is in good taste; Paul *will* like that. This thought cheered her up.

At noon, she hailed a taxi and sped off for her luncheon date. Arriving at the restaurant, she was glad to see that Jack and Susan had gotten there first. Ellie's French was uncertain. This way she could go to their table without having to make inquiries. Susan waved gaily, beckoning her over. She stood up, gave Ellie a hug and kissed the air near her ear. Ellie started to shake hands with Jack, but he came around the table, gave her a big hug and pulled out her chair for her.

"Ellie, I hope you don't mind. We know this restaurant well and took the liberty of ordering for you," Susan said. She didn't wait for an answer, but launched into a blow-by-blow description of all the treatments she was anticipating during the afternoon.

Ellie concentrated on the food, interjecting appropriate expressions of enthusiasm from time to time. Unused to having wine at lunch, she was feeling mellow. So Susan could afford a spa, so what. Jack said almost nothing. Every once in a while he would make eye contact with Ellie, his expression conveying the impression that they were complicit in indulging Susan.

Susan left in a rush to keep her appointment. Jack paid the check, said lunch was his treat, helped Ellie with her coat and soon they were in a taxi on the way to the Louvre.

Jack said they didn't need to hire a guide, and indeed they didn't. He proved to be very knowledgeable and gave her a personal tour of all the major works that tourists wish to see. He guided her by her elbow and offered his arm up and down stairways.

When they reached the Mona Lisa, Ellie couldn't contain her disappointment.

"Oh, no," she said. "Look, she's behind glass."

"It's bullet proof," Jack explained.

"But she's so far away."

"Yes, they won't let anyone get closer than this. She's such a treasure." Jack said this with a slight smile on his face, looking directly into Ellie's eyes.

Shortly after three o'clock, Ellie took a bathroom break and used a pay phone to call her hotel and leave a message for Paul, saying to meet the three of them for drinks at six, and giving the address.

When she returned, Jack surprised her by guiding her to the coat-check room near the entrance, saying, "Enough culture for one afternoon. It's time for a drink. I know a little bistro I think you'll like."

"Aren't we meeting Susan and Paul for drinks before dinner?"

"Yes, but your feet must be tired after all that tramping around on marble floors. We can have a little respite and a quiet chat. No more art talk."

Ellie's new shoes *were* pinching. A bistro! So French! She would feel like she was really in Paris; she acquiesced.

Ellie loved the little restaurant. Tucked in a side street, it was quiet. The bartender, who seemed to know Jack, greeted him effusively. The conversations were in French, no American tourists. Ellie felt cosmopolitan.

Jack ordered wine and chatted easily, touching Ellie's arm now and then to make a point. She began to think that she was quite the conversationalist, too. He ordered a second glass of wine, which Ellie didn't want. Engrossed in what Jack was saying, after a while she realized time was slipping by quickly. These French bistros seemed intimate, so cozy. Glancing down at her watch, she discovered Jack's hand covering hers; he was playing with her fingers as he talked. Somehow his touch had seemed natural and warm; she hadn't focused on what was happening.

"Susan and I have a rather grand suite in our hotel. We were lucky and were given an upgrade. Wouldn't you like to see it?" Jack asked.

"What, now? We have to meet the others."

"We have plenty of time." His tone was light, but coaxing.

Ellie regarded Jack with sudden insight, looked down at her hand entwined with his, reacted as if it belonged to a stranger, and withdrew it. She raised her arm, making a show of checking her wristwatch. "Oh, Jack, it's such a beautiful day and this is Paris. Can't we walk around for a little while? You can point things out to me, and then it will be time for us to meet Paul and Susan. Your wife will be gorgeous after those spa treatments."

"Are you quite sure?" he asked, recapturing her hand and gently kissing her palm. "It would be most enjoyable, you know."

Ellie blushed. "It probably would, but yes, I'm sure." Jack gave a little shrug of defeat as she reclaimed her hand.

At dinner Jack continued to be attentive, though of course there was no hand holding. Busy regaling the table with witty stories of misadventures in various foreign countries, Susan didn't notice.

Paul did notice, however. He reached under the table and took Ellie's hand, whispering, "You look especially pretty tonight." From Paul, this was a glowing tribute.

That night, as they were getting ready for bed, Paul took Ellie in his arms. "I truly do love you, you know," he said.

"I know you do," Ellie answered.

Paul got into bed with a sheaf of papers to review for tomorrow's business meeting. "Seeing Jack and Susan tomorrow?" he asked. It was a casual question, but Ellie detected the undercurrent of concern.

"No, I prefer to be on my own," she replied.

In the bathroom, Ellie brushed her teeth and then took the little round case containing her birth control pills from her toilet bag. She stared at the case for several minutes, then returned it to the bag. Spontaneity is often a good thing, Ellie thought. Serendipity has its rewards. ■

A Relationship to Treasure

Ker plip, ker plop. Ker plip, ker plop. Noah and I have pinged for pong to determine who will serve. As the game begins, the hollow ball hits against the long green table and our ping-pong paddles like the syncopated tapping of a woodpecker. It echoes through the room, the only sound breaking the silence as we concentrate on the game. The heads of onlookers turn back and forth, back and forth, until the ball hits the edge of the table and ricochets to the side. My nine-year-old grandson dives for the ball and misses; the room explodes with laughter. "Great point!" he exclaims, consoled by the substantial lead he has after the first point. "One to ten," he says as he retrieves the elusive ball and throws it my way.

At this moment he has a determined ambition--to beat his grandmother five years sooner than his father did as a boy. "You continue to play like this and you can forget about that lead." I smile and zing a surprise serve down the edge of the table to his backhand.

"Hey, no fair." He shakes his head, his once abundant dark hair now a short buzz. He is growing up and emulating the bald heads of his favorite basketball stars.

As I concentrate on moving the ball from side to side, from one edge of the table to the other, vivid pictures play in my mind--a little boy on the shore in Maine trotting up every morning from his cabin to ours. His mother released him at the bottom of the hill. We received him at the top. It was a fond ritual.

His grandfather and I have competed over the years to see which of us could offer him the most enticing entertainment. When he was two years old, I took him to our beach and taught him the pleasure of throwing stones into the water, hearing a resounding plop and watching the splash rise from the surface. He brought the larger stones to me and clapped with glee when I hurled them into deeper water than he could reach with his small arms. As the stones near him disappeared, he reached out chubby little hands. I obliged, hustling around the beach gathering more.

He threw each one with abandon, looking at me for approval when one made a large splash. His repeated, "More, please," left no doubt that the venture was a success.

In my mind it was "our thing," but when my husband started taking him to the beach, it became "their thing." At Christmastime we received a talking picture of him and his grandpa at the water's edge. When I pressed the button, he said in his two-year-old voice, "I love you, Peapaw, and I love to throw rocks." It still sits on my dresser and I cherish it, having relinquished the idea that it was "our thing."

The next summer we met his family in Bangor. "Well, hello, Noah!" my husband bellowed across the airport. Scooping up our grandson, "Peapaw" kissed his puckered lips and made whirring sounds like a motor against his neck. Noah giggled and dropped to the floor to play cars. His grandfather, ignoring the travelers all around him, crawled on his hands and knees making "little boy" noises: cars crashing, wheels screeching. Noah wanted Peapaw to sit next to him in the car.

My time will come, I thought, when Noah finds the present I bought him. When we reached the cabin, my husband grabbed the big red ladybug I left on Noah's pillow and rubbed its velvety softness on Noah's cheeks. He hugged it with delight.

That wasn't fair, that was mine to give him. I pouted like a child while Noah and Peapaw raced down to the shore to throw rocks in the water.

The next day Noah and I cuddled together inside the never used fireplace of our newly built cabin. I tied an old bobbin to a fishing line, threw the line over the hearth and reeled it in as I told him a fish story. He clapped his little hands and exclaimed, "Tell it again, Peapom!"

His smiling face radiant, he listened intently as I gave each story a new twist. "Tell it again, Peapom!" he cried each time the story ended. Two hours later, when his mother called him for his noon meal, Noah turned to me, his big brown eyes wide and pleading, "Peapom, can we do it again after lunch?" Nearly exhausted, I told him it was Peapaw's turn to play with him. Running to his mother, his lower lip quivering, his dark eyes brimming with tears, he stuttered, "She-she doesn't want to."

His time with me was as precious as his time with his grandfather! "Dear Lord, forgive my foolish heart, and thank You that he loves his grandfather."

From the time he was born, his mother made sure we saw Noah four times a year. One was always a summer visit to our island home in Maine. Over the years he ventured further out on the rocks and reached deeper into the cold water to pry loose the starfish we gathered along the shore together. He stocked our large tidal pool and after dark summoned us to accompany him with flashlights to watch the starfish crawl out from under rocks and move across the pool, safe from the gulls who fish there in the daytime.

Since he was a toddler, he has played with live lobsters before we cooked and ate them. After they became his pets, he wanted no part of eating them. Now that he is nine, however, he courageously tried one claw and, to everyone's surprise, asked for a second. We suspect he didn't want any island adventure to elude him.

According to his mother, this year when the plane came out of the clouds and he saw the coastal islands beneath him, he turned to her and said, "Mom, I love this place so much!" This past spring she had asked him, "If you could go anywhere in the world, where would you want to go?"

"Oh, Mommy, Maine! I just love it there." An only child, he was excited to be bringing friends with him for the first time, E. J. and E. J.'s two sisters and mother. The mothers and children of the two families toured the state for several days before their fathers joined them. "When are we going to get there, Mom?" he kept asking as though the rest of the state did not qualify as Maine. But when they arrived at our cove on Deer Isle, Noah was ecstatic with anticipation and thrilled to show every rock and trail to his guests.

His grandfather and I had agreed he was old enough to learn to row a boat. We had bought a Walker-Bay dinghy several years ago, but it was stolen the first summer we had it. Discouraged, we did not replace it. Now, excited by the thought of the fun he and his buddies would have rowing in our cove at high tide, we drove to Searsport to buy another one. Before we gave it to him, we asked his mother if she would be comfortable with that. She was delighted. Noah had been asking when he could learn to run our motorboat and how old he had to be to take it out on his own. His father had told him that as a boy he had learned to use a rowboat first and that was the place to start. Our daughter-in-law thought it was an inspired decision.

We gave the boat to him the morning after he arrived. Noah and his grandfather, with E. J. and his youngest sister Samantha, installed the seats and oarlocks. Noah didn't say much but the grin on his face told us he was excited. When the boat was finished, they all carried it down the hill to the water to launch it. Peapaw walked along the shore, instructing each child in turn how to row. It was a struggle at first, but by the end of the second day, each of the children could handle the boat with ease.

From their first exclamations, "This is fun!" to their happy calls across the cove and their eagerness to have a turn, we could tell the boat was a hit. At breakfast the third day, Noah said to his mom, "It's great being out there on the water alone, Mom."

That afternoon Noah, E. J. and Samantha rowed across the water and landed on the opposite shore near the creek that emptied into our cove. Their imaginations running freely, they played "pioneer," each setting up camp on a rock that was only half covered by the tide. With twigs and stones and bits of seaweed, they fashioned farms that produced crops and villages that made products, all of which they bartered back and forth.

Noah's body trembled from hours of standing knee-deep in cold water, but he was so intent on their trading game, he resisted his mother's first calls that it was time to row back. In spite of the warm shower, he remained cold all evening, but his bright eyes danced. The next morning his mother caught him grinning at the breakfast table and reported to me that he was enjoying every bit of his vacation.

Now that he has become more independent, my husband and I miss his slipping his hand into ours and pleading for us to accompany him on a starfish hunt at low tide or to collect stones on the beach. He no longer throws stones into the water; now he skips them on top. We count the skips of each stone as we watch them skim the surface. He is developing a strong arm and the skill of one who has practiced the art over and over again. I rejoice that he still calls out, "Watch this one, Peapom."

I miss his eager request to tell him a story. Instead I enjoy searching for books to feed his insatiable appetite for reading.

For two weeks Noah and E. J. collected washed-up crab and lobster claws on the beaches, pieces of driftwood, feathers, brightly colored rocks, shells and assorted treasures. On their last day they came to us to make a presentation. Noah spoke for them both, his smiling face becoming serious as he tried to convey the urgency of the need. "We decided our treasures would be popular in Dallas and we could sell them to make money. At first we thought of all the things we could buy with the money we earned, but I realized we were being selfish. There are so many children in the world who don't have all the great things we have, we decided to send the money we raise to an orphanage in the Ukraine!"

He paused and waited for our reaction. We knew that orphans were on his mind because his parents are in the process of adopting a Russian child. "Will you help us with the postage to send these things home, Peapom and Peapaw?"

"Of course, we would be happy to." The two of them broke into smiles and began making ambitious plans. E. J.'s two sisters bought rocks and shells for gifts with the money they had earned collecting discarded bottles and turning them in for recycling. Then the boys approached the adults. Before they left, they had raised $26.00. By making presentations to social gatherings and churches at home in Dallas, they have raised enough to feed 25 orphans two meals a day for four months. They are now searching for new ways to add to their fund. An entrepreneurial fire has been sparked, but even better, the desire to give back has become their goal.

Ker plip, ker plop, ker plip, ker plop. Our ping-pong games are becoming more and more fun as Noah's skills increase. This summer I won one game with only three points to spare. My time as ping-pong queen is growing shorter. Soon we will have a fine new champion, one who will achieve his ambition of beating his grandmother five years sooner than his father beat his mother. ■

Summer

It is summer, time to return to the land of poignant memory. At the Bangor airport I retrieve my luggage and take a taxi to the garage where I parked my 33-year-old station wagon last fall. After reconnecting the battery, I settle behind the wheel and turn the ignition key. "Please, let it start," I plead, my neck and stomach taut. With the roar of the engine, the tension relaxes. "Thank you, thank you." My eyes turn skyward, then back again to the pitted surface of my car which looks as if it has been attacked by acid rain. Rust patches decorate the light blue body like orange clouds in a sunset sky. Aware that my car will not last forever, I make a mental note to seek an alternative shelter from the harsh Maine winter.

I descend the long cement ramp leading into Bangor's crowded business section, cross the bridge over the Penobscot River and escape the city. As I pass green yards with blossoming shrubs, my summer adventure begins. Rhododendrons are in full bloom, their abundant pink-red and purple flowers heralding the year's longest day. Evergreens are a welcome contrast to the palm trees and sand that dominate my winter vistas.

I strain to catch every glimpse of the river. Birds glide lazily in the sky. I sigh and feel the pace of life slow. "Summertime and the living is easy, fish are jumpin'…" If only they would swim again in our bay! The disappearance of the flounder and pollack that once filled the waters in front of our cabin is the greatest change we have experienced in a lifetime of summers here. No one is sure why the fish left, but people speculate that it was pollution from chemicals dumped into the water by the paper mills and the loss of the eel-grass on which they fed.

In Penobscot I begin to see saltwater inlets pushing against the tree-lined shore. I pass Milton's Dream, a seafood take-out with a large pavilion on top of a hill overlooking scenic fields and woods. It was the site of many arriving and departing meals, where my family enjoyed the first and last lobster or crab rolls of the season. No food having been served on the long flight, my taste buds scream for attention but I do not stop. I yearn to reach what I have traveled so far to see.

As the car chugs up Caterpillar Hill, my heart races with anticipation. We crest the hill and I am awed. Penobscot Bay stretches before me as far as I can see. I pull into the overlook and open the door. A panorama of sparkling blue and green greets me: hundreds of green spruce-covered islands fill the bay whose water reflects the bright blue of the sky. The white sails of a few scattered boats dot its surface. Soon stately schooners carrying summer tourists will weave among them. Across the bay, the purplish hue of the Camden Hills adds a dimension of mystery.

I revel in the beauty of a crystal clear day. Moments like these draw me back year after year and make the long journeys from the southern tip of Florida worth the effort.

It is hard to believe that a bay so beautiful can become turbulent, its cold waters sometimes claiming the lives of expert fishermen. But today the bay promises adventure. Familiar landmarks in the distance remind me of happy excursions in my youth, boat trips repeated with children and now grandchildren.

Reluctantly, I climb back into my car. The bay disappears behind rolling barrens of low bush blueberries which will turn bright red in the fall. The old farmhouse that stood halfway down the hill has burned down, but I can see it still: isolated, bleak in its grayness, slowly deteriorating. The children called it haunted, but I wondered about the people who had lived there. Had they purposely given up that spectacular view and moved away or had their time simply passed with no offspring to carry on what they had started? For a fleeting moment I realize that I, too, will soon be gone and new generations will be drawn here.

As my station wagon climbs the towering Deer Isle - Sedgwick Bridge, I strain to see over its side rail. Halfway across, the water comes back into sight revealing Eggemoggin Reach nearing low tide. Herring gulls soar in all directions. Squawking loudly, they make interlocking white circles against the blue sky perhaps anticipating a feeding of castoffs from a returning lobster boat or a feast of the sea life soon to be exposed at low tide.

Descending the steep bridge onto Little Deer Isle, I open the window and breathe in the fragrance of the forest. As I cross the causeway from Little Deer to Deer Isle, the pungent smell of clam flats ushers in a rush of memories: digging clams with my father in our family cove, rolling them in saltwater to clean them and covering them with seaweed until meal time; years later, shelling cooked clams, swishing them in clam broth, dipping them in hot melted butter and, like a mother bird, popping them into the open mouths of my four children.

How I have loved this beautiful land, perpetually the same, yet ever changing with the tides and seasons. Without its influence, I would have grown up a city girl, but the enticements of the bay re-fashioned me into a lover of nature. All my life, the giant boulders and craggy ravines of its ragged coastline fascinated me; its varied moods intrigued me.

As a toddler, learning to walk on the granite coast developed perseverance, a determination to overcome all obstacles. Later, Maine's familiar foggy days reflected the brooding moods of my early teen years. On sunny days I climbed the rocky cliffs, watching the sparkle of a million diamonds dance on the surface of the sea. These birthed gratitude and enthusiasm and sudden bursts of spontaneity. The game of charades, played with my family before the roaring fire in the great stone fireplace my father built, taught me the fun of friendly competition. The silly antics we offered under pressure, acting out our assignments, drew laughter from deep within. Roasting marshmallows on glowing embers taught me patience as I slowly turned each one round and round toasting it to golden brown perfection.

I pass Burnt Cove filled with fishing and sailing boats lying peacefully at anchor. Not a ripple stirs the water. The many vessels sit motionless as though glued to a glass mirror.

I turn the car onto a small dirt road between two granite posts and I see myself through the years picking wild berries along its roadsides: the June strawberries tiny but sweet; July raspberries pure delight; August blueberries perfect for plump muffins smothered in butter; blackberries signaling the coming of fall.

I park the car near our cabin. The stream beside it is full, rushing out of the woods and through the middle of the cove now emptied by the tide, a changeless scene throughout my lifetime. I run to Sunset Rock, the twenty foot almost vertical stretch of granite in front of our cabin. As we waited for the sun to descend over Fifield Point, the children in the family ran up and down its steep face, causing the hearts of generations of mothers to pound with fear. But even the children stopped to watch the flaming red ball in the sky disappear behind trees across the bay and the sky turn festive shades of yellow, orange, pink and purple in the brilliant afterglow.

I step out on the rock, "Oh, no!" I close my eyes, denying the unwelcome sight. Shock trembles through my body. Tears well up and spill down my cheeks. The lone tree on the point that had kept vigil over the cove all the years of my life, lies prone on the cold granite, its branches rising from the trunk as if still alive except at its shriveled top. The lower part of its trunk is securely entrenched in a crevice in the rocks, but it is stark and jagged now. The fierce winds coming off the water which have bowed it over the years have snapped it and claimed its life.

I have lost a dear friend. This tree has been the constant in our view. Every year we said with affection, "The tree on the point is still there. Nothing ever changes." When I was a child, my family picnicked on the beach near it. I ate my food under its branches. I met my first love under that tree. Through all the generations, it was our meeting place whenever we planned a boat trip. When we approached our cove from the water, that single tree on the point, spotted from far away, assured us we were close to home.

Like the house on Caterpillar Hill and the fish in the bay, the tree is gone, but already a seedling is pushing up nearby to take its place. The island called The Fort that is the focus of our view has been barren most of my life. Twenty years ago small seedlings took root. As they grew and multiplied, it began to look like other tree-covered islands, but it is beautiful with or without trees. The tall island still stands sentinel to the entrance of our part of the bay and our view is still breath-taking.

Soon I will be as fragile and vulnerable as the tree on the point. But if I share my memories, what has come before will remain and become part of the experience of oncoming generations. The busy tide brings a multitude of daily changes; but the tide, itself, is as constant as the granite formations it exposes and covers. A love as deep as mine for this beautiful part of God's creation will not die with me. Through my children and grandchildren, it will endure. ■

David Hayman

Equestrian

She says she always loved horses
Kept a stable of plastic beasts in her room
Called herself cowboy, yes, I remember that
We have a photo of her kneeling over a cat
Watching it dispatch a sparrow hawk
On the back of her head a little straw thing

Didn't stop her producing and loving
Two boys who don't much like horses

Now in finance she has a 'farm,' a barn
Paddocks and stalls, six horses that she rides
Curries, mucks out for, feeds, nurses, to relax
Her Rolodex she says makes her valuable
Important people will answer when she calls

Still, young, youthful, athletic, charming
She rides, an Amazon, controlling with
Amply muscled thighs reluctant horses
Erect, girlish, giving as she takes
My daughter with whom I quarrel
Amiably as in her youth, the girl
We never needed to control because
She knew better than we the risks she ran
Even when she told us she was sharing
Her dorm bed with a pigtailed Chinese boy
Or when she found her "blond Adonis"
Left sculpture for publishing for Wall Street

She's always risked and always won
Raised herself in our image without our help

We weren't always friends
My first baby, she rejected me for my wife
Then I rejected her
We competed for food and affection
Once I left her at a friend's house
Just drove off, knew her absence
Only when I turned to show her a horse
Grazing in the northern California field
Not deliberate, no, but not good either
Then she won me, charmed me with her quirks
Taught me to worry about, to respect and then
to love the freedom of her spirit

 And now she rides

David Hayman

Memory Mines

Mornings, as I slowly wake,
Gathering up diminished force,
Occulted items elbow for place,
Spontaneously coalescing into,
Not one or two, but multitudes.

Recollections of accidents exhume
The shitty pants, the rock that gashed
My infant skull, near fatal stings,
My first bicycle colliding with that car,
Slipping and the sound of shattered bone.
A wet Maine night and head-on crash,

Events of moment years apart,
Accompanied by their occasions,
By galaxies of thoughts and feelings,
By consequences, shock and pain.
Seeds planted in the loam of memory
Sprout fresh, produce rank weeds
And occasional lavish blooms.

And what of sex, as that Freshman wrote,
"From infancy to adultery," a catalogue:
That schoolboy's toes nudged my genitalia,
The bathtub explorations, the random touch,
Those bus rides, uncontrollable excitation,
The feel of a girl's arm, the fumbling, the kiss,
The little Mexican whore who stopped
My probing paw, "That hurts!," and saw
Me through my first experience, inexpertly,
Those evenings in those hallways,
The Swedish girl whose landlord
Intervened, her ample breasts,
Seductions in the woods, on an island,
In full view, in my imagination, manifold,
The wedding night, the sleeping bag,
Nights on our narrow bed,

The final orgy, the last erection, residuals.
And from these ruins a life disjunct relived.

But these are incidentals.
What of the spirit?

Revelations,
That first Godawful poem,
That sheen of inspiration,
Composed in ignorance,
Scribbled on a scrap of paper,
In the HEAT OF THE MOMENT!
The serial disclosures made by paintings, found in books.
The chance meetings, unplanned conjunctions,
Pregnant intuitions, encountering Joyce,
Meeting Beckett, seeing clowns in San Luis.
Life-altering occasions, all, initiating what?
The next necessary step in an unexceptional life
Where sparkles serendipity.
Meeting the girl who is my wife.

Pull any strand, the rest unravels,
But not forever. Knots intervene,
Net you in a mesh of ambiguity.

Must I go on interminably
Fleshing out occasion with detail
The clown of my diversity
Tumbling endlessly
In my soiled linens
Through distinctions that won't hold
Because I can't untie the knots,
Cannot imagine definition
Less than ultimate,
Can't see life whole,
Eliminate pulsation,

Even when I squash the spider in its web,
Dispose of chance, terminate in sleep my meditation,
Tear off covers, stand up, stretch,
Perform matutinal ablutions, and proceed,
Extending for the nonce,
My own life sentence?

David Hayman

The Peasants' Feast, Ibiza

On the other side of the island
The peasant feasters sat
Beneath extended eaves,
At a long table under the
Brilliant carbide lamp
That etched their faces
Lined or startled in their youth,

A long table for the great communal dish.
Only we "foresteros" had spoons and plates,
A courtesy, a sign of gratitude and mark of distance.
Bartolemeo and Maria our guarantors
Among impoverished fisher farmers
On the other side of the known, on the rocky shore
Across from Vedra, that island pyramid,
Great rock pasture for the summer flocks
Where that year we'd joined the chase.

Bartolomeo, blond accident in this dark country,
Leader with no authority, had caught that great fish,
Cooked and served it now, veteran and survivor.

We ate the light that evening savoring community,
Joining without belonging, tossing fish bones
Over shoulders for lean dogs to gobble,
Dogs starved to sharpen their taste for rabbits
Vestiges of ancient times, the same portrayed
In Roman sculpture, and on Egyptian tombs.

This is History's island after all,
Home to Carthaginians, Romans, Moors,
Perhaps that's why these hard bitten,
Independent, feuding folk
Are also warm and loyal friends, allies.

Before the Frankists, they were Loyalists.
Anticlerical, they'd burned their priest in his church.
Now in thrall to the Fascisti,
Reluctantly they licked the whip,
Paid taxes to support police and clergy.

Bartolemeo, wild spoor of passing Normans,
Let Maria tell Marie Helena, who told us
Of those times.

How Loyalists settled scores the island way.
How, when Fascisti came, there was retribution.
Spread out on their ungenerous lands,
These people were close in blood and they remembered.
Aiding "the enemy," no matter whose, endangered.

Surely it was the wrong moment
To have errands in that village,
And not the best time to help Jose,
The simpleton who'd mopped the barracks.
But it was the code. It was his nature.
He promised shelter, took that risk.

Their trail, the one we followed, was narrow, devious.
Someone betrayed them, some neighbor with a grudge.

The soldiers stopped them, bound them, led them back –
Part way. "Just to that dry river bed, near that bush,"
Marie Helena told us as we neared the farm,
"Then they told them, 'Stop! Now say your prayers.
You're going to die.' So he said, 'You're on your own!'
Hit that gully, running into country he knew best."
Maria didn't say how he survived,
With neighbors' help no doubt,
No doubt by stealth.

Between mouthfuls of fish and rice and sips of rough red wine,
I thought of this, watching faces glowing in that light
And wondering what those feasters did those years,
Who among them aided him, as he now aided them,
And how, through centuries of forgetting,
They and their hungry hounds survived.

David Hayman

Supposing Death

Yes
I'd lie there in the dark
Thinking
I will die
Some day
Shivering with dread
How could I end
That I
My little self
Inhabited
What could nothingness be

Deep physical dread
Tightened the skin
Around my flesh
It never failed
No escape
No immortality
Never
Only never
In the bones

Unremitting
Though intermittent
Death imposed itself
Age did not abate it
Nor the illusions of belief

Until
In old age
I found my mirror map
Watched with fascination
The slow accumulation of signs
Wrinkle here
Brown spot there
Till
The shape of my face
Would find
Its ultimate
Likeness.

David Hayman

Driving Home Last Night

This is the road I take,
The same hill I sweat up,
The same water viewed through foliage,
The same roadside vegetation,
Familiar byways, stones and weeds,
The causeway wriggling by in waterwise.

It is late enough and overcast.
My headlights, beamed on bright,
Enchant the roadside as we wind
Past the stones that mark my passage,
Turning huge clumps of intervening weeds
Into stage sets for a faerie pageant,
Faceting them, bejeweling them
Into brilliants various in green and gold,
A jungle set, a distant place
To light imagination's flares.

Passing now, into and through the trees,
Reshaping foliage, accenting trunks,
As we climb the slope I hardly know,
But know too well and know the turns
And know the slope and now,
With dangerous dark speed
We slide past neighbors' lights,
Estrangement dissipating into reassurance,
Mutating into disappointment like a sigh,
As we turn abruptly,
But with caution,
Up our drive.

Is home the place we want to be?
Of course, and tomorrow I'll forget,
See only road, wave my appreciation
At those cars that widen my walking way,
Breath heavily up the hill and mop my brow
With sidelong glances at the passing scene,
Another day, another
Constitutional.

Nancy B. Hodermarsky

A Large Copper Cow
Under a Small Watercolor
for Ron Stegall

When forged for a barn in Indiana,
did you bargain the fire, the bending, the hammering
into a beast with its back to the snow and the rain?
Or being nailed high on a beam in blistering sun?
Did you bargain the boy, the spinning 'round
from the gun, the willful winds riddling the wounds
in your neck, your breast, your flank, your udder?

A century later you find yourself,
inanimate still on a library shelf
a meadow above, not beneath you:
blue stream, dappled shallows, ripened fields
joined to the skies of a late afternoon,
those pink horizontals mirrored
with river grasses in slow flowing water.

Rise, dear cow, float, slip into couple-color,
that you may cross at the painting's edge
into life from its reflection. You will be whole,
a brindled cow, so sure of your pasture,
in pleasure with each herb and flower
while you wait for the boy to come whistling,
as he does at this hour,
to bring both of you home.

Nancy B. Hodermarsky

Hand in Hand

"Grandma, when did you begin
to walk so slow?" asks Andrezj.
We climb from the shore, hand in hand.
It is June, thieving birds among green leaves, and

I am a child, gladly on my knees,
tying a shoe under a cherry tree;
Grandfather, straight-backed in a three-piece suit,
straw hat, is unable to bend down.

"When you were born," I say,
"I carried you in my arms."
Andrezj nods, turns and tugs us up the rise.
Into his hands I commend myself.

Nancy B. Hodermarsky

Hurtgen Forest
Winter 1945

How cold, how foul these seeping roots,
this bedding down among blind worms
with sodden planks and clumps of earth.
Hail Mary, full of grace, ...
We are gambling for life, the medic and I,
in an improvised tomb, my fever, 105.
The air pipe is working. He has our supplies:
K-rations, batteries, canteens of water.
We will survive from dusk to dusk,
perhaps longer, in this underworld
dug by corporals.
Our Lord is with thee...
He has his brandy and all of my sulfa.
He sets the alarm every four hours.
Should I trust the drunken bastard
or shoot both of us now?
How soundly he snores.
I am curled round my rifle.
but I can't feel my guts.
I hear their shells whistling the falling,
know their trajectory's wrong,
and yet...we're dying.

Will they remember where they foxholed the forest
under Tiger Tanks and death-spattered Howitzers?
Will they search among the limbless,
frozen in ice, shrouded by snow?
No, we are the underearth, the medic and I,
the beginning and end of stones and rivers.
Holy Mary, ...Pray for us, sinners,
Now, and at the hour...

Nancy B. Hodermarsky

undersong

phantoms, apparitions
possess us unbidden
rising through water
dissolving in dusk
shadows in windrows
illusions on stairs
bearers of messages
split warnings
stringed intuitions
fathoms deep
deeper than instinct

riding vibrations of fire
into the night
they foul our ears
feast on our eyes
spin faster, leap deeper
louder cry
while flaying open
our blackened hearts

only at matins
a stillness comes
from slivered moons
truths of the bone
a grain of strength
on the tongue
opening for us
the bluest of doors
for a step, one step,
and beyond

Nancy B. Hodermarsky

The Warp of Desire

Months of cold, weeks of high wind,
grey skies, pale skies, a little rain
but not enough for the dry earth
of a palace where no one weeps,
where longing weaves into years
of unraveling.
For here in the hall I sit
at my loom divining
out of gaudy threads from the songs
they sing: wine-dark seas, lotus leaves,
one-eyed giants, witches, pigs,
clashing rocks and sirens' calls,
a princess with a golden ball.

Such tales the suitors string
from the notes of the lyre
and all these treacheries I will untell
before dawn while the palace sleeps.
All must fall to the floor before me
to be wound again into skeins
that will weave only the truth
into a shroud.

Soft now I trace with fingertips
upon the proud cliffs' rising,
upon the riven olive's
crippled clinging to its troubled heart.
Here, a river rushes down
to hide its cry in the deep
and there, on high, the prophetic eye
guides safe homecoming.
These are the tales
that will not be undone.

He will return, that man so full
of desire, one ever aroused
by sidelong smiles,
a lovely wrist, the flick
of a speaking tongue at the lips,
a hesitation in the turning.
He will return and I will sit
in my inlaid chair by a starved fire
among all my white-armed maids
questioning him, feigning distance.
He will lie and I will listen.
I will be quite still,
except for the tapping, so still,
a bare foot in a golden sandal,
beckoning...

Almanac Leaves

Rose hips are red,
blueberries few,
small wild cranberries sleep
under the dew…

II: (Haiku)
Autumn equinox
Soft air surrounds the cabin
Of the lobsterman

D Immonen

Back Behind Country Inn at the Mall

Her and I walked up the road —
Nevah been theah befoah
Up past a empty lot
Then a new HomeanHahrth….
Piles of fiberboahd outside
Behind the Mecca Mall

On the left side of that road
Three small oldish houses
Flower in mightycareful plots
Lots of rocks
Them yellazinyas probly do well
Come late August

What's our goal when we
Nevah have walked a particular road?
That fancy halcyonstreetlight
Still on at eight a.m.?
We passed that by….

Well we kept walkin'
On up to the top of the hill
And blam… another road cuttin' off to the left —
Grinly Ridge, I believe it was

Theah was a sign right theah
AUTHORIZED PERSONELLE ONLY

We looked at each other, sister and me
"Well," says sister,
"We may not be au-tho-rized
But we sure as hell
Are person-elles…
Now let's
Jog on back"

Mixed Messages Re: Joyce

Thesaurus calumny.
Gossips sitting isolated
on uncomfortable chairs.
Was is this Ulysses great?
How great, Irish hearth grate, harp
green spring soap would she take a bath?
Did her baby now lost take/receive baths
(photos remembered)

Seriously think but willcannot share this
speculajoyce hieratic silliness — footnote:
speculative silliness.
Joycestreamofconsciousness with
linebreaks imposed by   computer why did anyone ever
involved in this claptrap hokkyhuggermuggery?
Different versions, minor variations
Myownpersonal favorite, dark red realhard book, this,
Bought   secondhand belonged to one Gail McDowell,
but that's not relevant though the Mc
Dowell colony is for artists, and artists and musicians
need to get a way, even in eden
can they turn off all the thoughts? or just edit

Not a lot of questionmarks inJoyce —
Maybe we, every Thursday night in island summers,
become inverted question marks like Spinoza?
Obscure reference to another bit of fun rollicking
outside apartfrom perhaps never between the sheets
ua kiliapu maua i kanahele* that sits on the page   in any
versionot Spanish but avid.
Get to the heart of some vague reference: In

yes the deadmarch of Saul, snugsong in some irish popular
and Antonio has to be Vivaldi, but how about the
following rhyme word look it up
not now
need to start to look at fingerings from the Baroque,
and tune the trifocals in on measures as a whole.

THAT'S a goal
page ninety-six, sister
(ninety-seven in your copy.)

*Hawaiian for "two bellies in the bushes"

Most Celestial Activity

Suspended,
we stand, sweater-swathed,
in a maritime meadow
ringed with tall spruce

Seeking
unimaginable images
Stars so several
the dark extends

An astronomer
aims his flashlight
up into light years,
tracing ancient Chinese stories, Greek myths

While past particles of comet dust
signal celebration,
my right eye
gives its own light-splashing retina show

D Immonen

Sprung

Solemn sentry
a crow a tree
deep dark thrust
a love
once gone

        returns

Soft smile
this island mist
foghórn warning
thoughts
illusions

        blur

as a painter's fingerside
smooths charcoal

The Glass Jar

I woke slowly, not sure where I was. The dark curtain of the sky was punctuated with stars and a full moon hung low and orange. I must have fallen asleep on the chaise. I noticed that my book had fallen on the floor and I would have to search for the place where I had been reading.

Suddenly, I heard singing. It sounded like Bill singing and laughing that wonderful contagious laugh. It had been five years since he'd died; I must have been dreaming. The moon was shining on something in the yard, sparkling unnaturally bright. It was a glass jar. Quart size. Bill was in it, singing, "I've got you under my skin." He used to sing it to me. So sexy. Made me tingle in all my secret places. There were other people in the jar with him and when he laughed, they all laughed too. The Pied Piper of fun. They must be having a party. We used to have such swinging parties with all the musicians, our friends. Many of them were professionals, some, like Bill, just very good amateurs. There was one problem: too many drummers, and only one drum set (thank God). But when Louise got on the vibes, I often wished they let her be the drummer. She was terrible at playing the vibes.

The jar looked like it was shaking with the rhythm, the grasses undulating all around it. Oh, Bill, sing "Bill Bailey?" He really ripped that song apart. About 10:30 one evening at the beach, a group of us decided to have a parade down Bay Avenue. Don had his trumpet, Frank his clarinet, someone was banging on a snare drum. The rest of us marched along behind them singing "Won't you come home Bill Bailey?" Quite a rouser. As we moved down the road, people started coming out of their houses, clapping and some of them joined us. Of course, there were a few "Shut the hell up!"'s that emitted from dark bedroom windows. When we got to the pavilion, everyone crowded around and Bill jumped up on the railing that encircled it. Holding onto the pillar, he sang a magnificent solo rendition. Everyone hooted and clapped.

"We better clear out of here or somebody is gonna call the police." someone said.

I laughed, "Oh, don't worry about that. The chief of police was one of Bill's best friends when they were in school together."

I closed my eyes and then opened them slowly. The jar was still there. What was going on? Was I losing it after eighty years? Or was this just a dream that would go away soon? Bill was climbing a mountain, his back to me. I recognized his dark hair, broad shoulders and no butt. So that may have been the time on our honeymoon in the mountains of western North Carolina. Someone had told him there was a high watch tower at the top of this mountain with a fantastic view of half of the United States and he had insisted that we should climb it. Reluctantly, I huffed and puffed behind him (that being the first mountain that I had ever climbed — and, I might add, the LAST!). When we reached the top, we could not see the watch tower through the fog, but when we finally did find it, there were only chunks of burnt wood strewn around in weeds. Someone told us later that it had burned down the year before. Back at the car, we discovered there was a flat tire.

In addition to our suitcases, the car was filled with boxes of birthday presents for me, including a full set of dishes and a large antique lamp. To get to the spare tire, everything had to be unpacked. Later, we laughed about that adventure but, at the time, it was late and getting dark and didn't seem so funny.

The jar is emitting a different sound. It sounds like Bill but the voice is angry. I first saw him lose his temper when we had been married almost four years. Early one morning, he came into the bedroom. I had just gotten out of bed and was wandering around in my nightgown. Something had set him off: I don't remember what it was I did to cause him such irritation. At the time, I thought he was kidding me. I'd never experienced his anger before. So, I willingly went along with what I surmised was a game and started to giggle. At first, he couldn't believe my reaction to his rage. How could I be so uncaring? Then he looked down at me, started laughing and put his arms around me.

The fireflies were spritzing the night with green-gold and several moths were attracted to the light in the jar. I heard music again; this time, it was in Cody, Wyoming at Jim and Hilda's. Jim had been Bill's copilot in the Mediterranean during the Second World War. He and his wife had bought an old spa on the Shoshone River, outside of Cody. It had a sulfur spring which had been made into a swimming pool. Older people with older peoples' aches and pains used to come to the spa and swim in the water, hoping to be cured. Before Jim and Hilda bought it, the former owners had turned it into a restaurant and night club, called "The Bronze Boot." Jim was a wizard on the piano and also played a jazz organ. Some great music pushed out the walls of that building every night. Old Arnie was on bass, Uncle Irontail on guitar and sometimes there was a clarinet player. They played the "big band music" that was so popular during the war and into the fifties, and a lot of jazz. Uncle Irontail also played country western on a wild banjo. The summer we went out to visit, Bill had his drum set shipped out, so he could join the group. He also sang with them and I loved to listen to him. I thought he was almost as good as Frank Sinatra, but definitely not as rich. I hopped tables and had a great time talking to those westerners in their cowboy boots — both the men and women — and their hundred-dollar custom-fitted jeans. Sometimes sheep herders, with scruffy beards and no designer jeans, were there, down from the mountains. The Mayor of the town came often, each night with a different woman. The fellows used to take bets on which one he would show up with on any given night. During the daytime, while everyone was busy getting things ready for the evening shindig, Bill and I would wander around town and drive up into the mountains. Huge rock faces dominated the landscape and a multicolored pallet of flowers spread across the sunny fields. Bill had lived with Jim and Hilda for nine months after the war, helping them to get the restaurant in shape and he still knew a lot of people in Cody.

VROOM! VROOM! VROOM! When I heard that sound emitting from the jar, I knew exactly what was coming next. I could see Bill in a crouched position, almost sitting on the back of his heels, his arms pumping wildly, his body moving only backwards. This was his "Italian tank" routine; the joke being that an Italian tank could only operate in reverse. He always put this act on for Claudette, my brother's wife, who was Italian. The more she laughed, the more he would perform. VROOM!

The four of us were staying in the Pocono Mountains one weekend. One day, we drove into town to get some wine. It was midmorning and although none of us had had anything to drink, Bill went into his Italian tank routine on the pavement before we went into the liquor store. As we entered, we were all laughing foolishly. The man behind the counter refused to sell us anything.

"You've already had enough!" he growled at us.

I began to hear music again but this time it was muffled. Bill was climbing up a ladder which leaned against the old maple tree in our back yard. We had bought a two-hundred-year-old farmhouse on seven acres in the country and were in the process of extensively renovating it. Bill was busy tearing out walls and building new ones, including a floor-to-ceiling fireplace wall out of brick in the kitchen. I was busy building a baby. With the kitchen finished and a baby girl in the nursery, we decided to have a party to celebrate.

The Glass Jar

Early in the spring, Bill had put a speaker in the top of the maple tree so that he could have music when he was working outside in his garden. Just before the guests were supposed to arrive, he got his jazz records together and turned on the speaker. Bizarre sounds emitted from it. He got the extension ladder from the workshop and when he climbed to the top, discovered a robin's nest with four blue eggs in the recessed part of the speaker. Off on another branch, was an extremely agitated mama robin. Bill came down, turned off the speaker and put the ladder away. The music would have to come from a different source for that party.

I heard him singing again, holding the microphone, standing with his knees slightly bent. This time the he sang "Body and Soul." So great to hear it again.

A thought suddenly shot through my head like a sizzling firecracker.

"If he can be in that jar, why can't I? Then we could be together again. How can I get myself in there?" I stood up, closed my eyes. There was a strong breeze. Cooling. Then it was gone. I opened my eyes and realized with excitement that I was in the jar. I was actually inside the jar! But, where was Bill? Where were all the people and places that I had been revisiting? There was no one anywhere. No one! How could this be happening? "Bill! Honey! Where are you?"

Suddenly, I heard a tapping on the side of the jar. I turned toward it. There, its pale, iridescent wings flickering in the light, was a luna moth. Trying to get in. ■

Isle au Haut High

Our skin the color of summer
we gathered berries
in paper cups.
Surrounded by a bowl of blue,
blue sky,
blue bay,
far as we could see.
In a field of warm grasses
blueberry juice sweet on our lips,
we made love.

Memorial

July 2nd
Edged by rusty, iron fences,
the cemetery stones, covered with moss,
choked by high grasses and artificial flowers,
sit forgotten.

July 3rd
Two men weave between the stones,
manicuring grass and weeds
to give the cemetery
a temporary air of respectability.

July 4th
American flags and geraniums
decorate the graves.
Bones lie beneath,
not caring.

No Whispers

No whispers from the trees today.
The cove so still, it mirrors
the rocks along the shore.
A white skiff drifts by,
leaving little wake.

My memory bones
conjure up other times
of white caps dancing ,
sun, inside and out,
water play and laughter.

It's eighty-eight degrees
in the shade of my porch.
How cool to be drifting
in a white skiff,
going nowhere.

The Survivor

She leaned across the table
and wiped it clean with a damp cloth.
Wearing a white T-shirt,
it was obvious that
she had only one breast.
With no bra, it wobbled
from side to side
and up and down
whenever she moved.
If she stood up straight,
her solo breast was pendulous.

"Can I take your order now?"

I wondered about all the days
she had lived through
to become a survivor.
Had there been someone
to hold her hand?
To drive her back and forth?
To laugh with her when she laughed?
To wrap around her when she cried?
To sing love songs to her?

A Sensitive Predicament

A man approached me as I left the Municipal Building and introduced himself as Bruce. We were carrying matching packets of paperwork from the Human Resource Department and realized both of us were hired as staff for the new drug program.

"Why do you think we aren't being told where the center is going to be located?" he asked.

"I don't know. They sidestepped the answer to that question when I asked."

Bruce suggested we carpool to the staff meeting the next morning. The forty-five minute drive from Ann Arbor would give us an opportunity to share what we knew.

A drug detoxification center was going to open somewhere in Garden City. We were to meet in the Municipal building until we moved. There didn't seem to be a lot more information to share, we admitted, as we pulled into the parking lot and prepared to attend our first staff meeting.

Our director, Paul, introduced the staff and announced, much to my surprise, that I was to be head nurse and Bruce was the program's head social worker. Two social workers and our physician would join us within the month. Paul assured us it wouldn't be too much longer before we could move into our new building.

"Wherever that is," I murmured to Bruce as Paul started to recite an overview of what we were recruited to do.

What a project! The staff was given a mandate to design an outpatient barbiturate detoxification program, the only one of its kind east of the Mississippi.

Barbiturate detoxification is very difficult, may often be a cause of death and is usually done in a hospital setting. This job would require all of my nursing and administrative skills. It promised to be quite a challenge.

We continued to meet in the Municipal Building to discuss policy and treatment goals. Each week we heard we were getting closer to moving into our facility. I asked if I could look at the space so I could order medical equipment and supplies. Paul shook his head.

"It's a political situation, a very sensitive predicament," he said.

"A very secret predicament," I murmured to Bruce. "Who are these politicians?"

I heard a ghoulish voice beside me say, "Who knows? It's a sensitive, secret, political predicament." I didn't dare look at Bruce. He would have kept me laughing if I had.

"Now would be a good time for you to go to the Haight-Ashbury Clinic." Paul pointed to me. "See me after the meeting."

Far be it for me to refuse a two-week trip to San Francisco. The Center would pay for my flight and be pleased it wouldn't have to pay for my lodging. It was a great time to visit with my brother, Bill and his family. My days would be spent observing the clinic's medical procedures, and I could have fun in the evenings.

September, a perfect month to be in San Francisco, is a little warmer than the rest of the year, making it more comfortable to walk up and down the hills of the city. My brother was concerned about my safety, so he insisted on walking me to and from the clinic. It was comforting to have his company, knowing he had been mugged in the "Haight" and his jaw wired for months.

The clinic was in a "painted lady" on the middle of a hill; light blue with rose and green trim. It was a striking old Victorian house. I walked up a long flight of stairs to the front door which opened into the reception area. A woman, who was sitting on a man's lap, greeted me, said I was expected and sent me down the hall to the nurses' office. I found out later that she was the receptionist and the lap of the man belonged to a client. I had never witnessed such conduct in a medical facility and doubted I'd permit this inappropriate behavior in *any* setting.

The nurses' office was next to their secure pharmacy in the back of the house. The day nurse took me on a tour of the rest of the building. Worn oriental rugs were everywhere, including the bathrooms. Old stuffed furniture and tasseled lampshades blended with the style of the house. Self-help books on various medical problems filled bookcases along one wall of the first floor. There were bulletin boards and colorful posters on the stairwell walls leading to the bedrooms on the second floor. These were now used as examining rooms and places for clients to rest. Counseling offices and storage space occupied the third.

Most of my time was spent on the second floor, observing the intake process and learning the guidelines to assess a client's history. This information was used to establish a decreasing medication schedule. *"This is serious business,"* crossed my mind more than once during the two weeks. There were many tense moments.

I found the setting to be quite different from any of my previous work environments. I enjoyed the warmth the staff expressed towards each other, but questioned their relaxed manner with the clients. I expressed my concern to Bill on our walk home one evening.

"The staff is very cozy with the clients."

"Well, Sis," Bill reminded me, "they *are* flower children, after all."

"We're in the 70s, not the 60s."

Bill laughed, "Yeah, but they may not know that."

The time went by very quickly. I received the medical information I needed and the health care staff promised to be available to me by phone. My visit with my family was an added bonus.

Bruce called me the day I returned to Michigan and said the township had finished negotiating with the owners of the building we were to occupy. We met the staff the next morning in a parking lot of a one-story, grey cinder block building on a main street in Garden City. *"This is not a San Francisco Painted Lady."* Paul brought us through the front door into a reception area. The door to the rest of the building was closed. *I wonder what is behind that door?* I perched on the window seat and introduced myself to the new personnel who'd arrived while I was away. Bruce sat next to me. A new social worker, on the other side of the room facing me was sitting on a man's lap. *"Don't tell me I have to deal with this activity here, too. I thought I had left this behind."* I raised my eyebrows at Bruce.

"Her boyfriend," he mouthed looking up at the ceiling.

Bruce whispered as he moved closer, "How do you like the décor?"

I tried not to laugh. The wall was covered in green and gold velvet flocked wallpaper and the shag rug was a strange shade of faded red.

"I wonder if the previous owners had some sort of Christmas business?" I mused.

The office manager asked us to move some dented metal desks and cabinets around to her liking, not an easy thing to do on a shag rug. Bruce grumbled about people thinking he could move furniture because he was so tall. He said his back resisted that sort of struggle. It sounded like a warning for any future moving requests.

Eventually, Paul opened the door to a long hallway that led to the only source of natural light, a window in the back door. More gold flocked wallpaper lined the walls and the faded red rug continued to the end of the hall. The place smelled dank and moldy.

We began to open the doors to the individual rooms.

I let out a whoop, "Ye gads!"

A Sensitive Predicament

Most of the rooms had gold etched, mirrored ceilings, reflecting red velvet flocked wallpaper; one wall was green. The floors were covered in dirty shag rugs. The kitchen was furnished with a greasy stove and stinking refrigerator. That wasn't the most astonishing sight: there was a large water bed on the floor in five of the seven rooms. Paul neglected to tell us that we were moving into a brothel. The "negotiating" was actually the eviction of the building's previous occupants.

A man with a stethoscope across his shoulders wandered down the hall. "I'll take a red room, but I don't want mirrors." Our physician had arrived. We laughed as he introduced himself,

"Call me John. We'll get along just fine." I made an appointment with him to go over our protocol.

We went back to the reception area to discuss the décor problems. *"This building is in sharp contrast to the Haight-Ashbury Clinic."* The budget for the program did not include renovations. None of our credentials included building repair, but obviously some things had to be done. The ceiling mirrors were tiles and could easily be removed. We could change the wallpaper one room at a time. But what, in heaven's name, were we going to do with the water beds? Water beds weigh a ton; we couldn't just pick them up and carry them out.

The next morning we arrived at work with pails in hand. None of us had any experience with water beds. We held our breath as the plug was pulled out of the corner of a bed. We were expecting a flood. Nothing happened. Three corners were lifted to tip the mattress towards Bruce, who was holding a pail near the unplugged hole. We laughed so hard we kept aiming away from the pail. Bruce tried moving the pail toward the moving hole without success.

"There has got to be a better way than this," croaked Bruce, as he sat on the floor, rolled over and hung onto his side laughing. We replaced the plug and decided we would do some research before coming to the center the next day.

We checked in with each other the next morning before coming to work and decided we would bring as many hoses to the center as we could find. Our first attempt was to siphon the water out the backdoor. The momentum of the water was not strong enough to keep it draining.

"I think I heard somewhere that water doesn't naturally run up hill."

"Thanks for telling us that, Paul," someone hollered from the backyard.

Now *we* were in a "sensitive and political predicament." After an hour of brainstorming, Paul asked what kind of impression the neighbors would have of us if we ran the water out the front door.

"It can't be any worse than what they had of the previous business," I responded.

"It's worth a try."

So, the next day we, once again, hooked up a hose to one of the beds. We lowered a corner of the bed while Bruce sucked up on the end of the hose to start the water flowing. I took the other end of the hose, ran through the hall, out the door, down an incline, and put it into the gutter.

Bruce and I spent the next two days sitting on the curb of the main thoroughfare watching the water flow under our knees and down the street. It was a fruitful time of sharing our philosophy of healthcare. We agreed that this adventure would add some levity to the very serious business we were about to undertake. We also understood the joy of contributing to a another person's welfare.

We didn't know it then, but we were destined to become lifelong friends. Years later we were still telling the story of the water beds in a brothel, and we laughed just as hard each time we told it. ■

David Lund

Descent in SoHo

We made our way in light rain,
It was after five — already night —
Where sheer dark streets
And assembled rows
Of cast-iron monarchs
Feigned indifference to us
In their velour tones.
Puddles glistened by our feet
As vapors rose above the sheen of stones,
Burnishing the antique streets
The hollow guttering of Prince and Greene.

Dark silvered mirrors tent the sky
And mica flashes
In the sealed gray corridors —
The windows, passages of glass
Are shuttered down
And even more aloof than before,
Except a solitary storefront,
Pane of light
To remind us not to care,
As if we could afford the glance,
Or fathom how to be marooned
Outside the illumined cube
From which sequined mannequins
Perfect their stare.

On a Scroll by Shih Tao

Imagine air   a spirit cloud   and spidery designs
     Spun of tendrils, incense-bearing shrubs,
         Waffled pillow stones
             Of pumice gray, trailing meadow grass,
                 Limbs of plum and cherry ripening
                 And floating bands of pearl
                 And orchid mist, where Lohan sages sway
         Their keenly threaded silks, vapor-edged,
     Exhale their iridescent breath, eyes rapt
With amazement and delight.

Imagine Lohans tread the saffron earth
     Besotted in the Buddha light,
         As rhythms braid the sinews of the stones
             To undulations in the dappled ground,
                 Echoing vibrato of the seers —
                 As then a burst of light
             Unveils the mythic creature
         In the garden's core: Dragon seething
     In celestial space, a coiling wraith,
The awe of avatars and saints,
Mouth of heaven's energy afire.
     As visions take their shape, unfurl
         Sages comb the atmospheres,
             Layers of the pearl —
                 Watching I draw near, in trance,
                 Enter the incomparable space.

Deborah Wedgwood Marshall

> _Pure, fresh, wholesome food will change philosophy,_
> _politics, economy and spirituality._
> —_Alice Waters_

O.C.S.C.

The Oral Climax Social Club was conceived the morning Princess woke up in the bed of Randy's parents. While he made coffee, she turned over and saw, on the bedside table, an interesting looking, delightfully aromatic pink envelope addressed to him. With her curiosity floating near the surface, she reached over and picked it up. She looked at the address and studied the handwriting, read the return and decided that "Sandi" who had written the letter, was a borderline illiterate. The writing was irregular and composed of both upper and lower case letters, something that always drove Princess nuts. She reached into the slit envelope and took out two pages of perfumed passion.

"Oh, my God!" she groaned. "This chick is over the top!"

The letter was mostly crap about Sandi's miserable life and her trouble with her mom, which was really trouble with herself. She had been grounded because she'd constantly missed her curfew. "A whiner," Princess labeled her. "Hmm...why the heck is she still living with her mom anyway? She must be around thirty. Randy is."

The last paragraph really got her: "Oh Randy," it said. "I miss you so much. Let me know when you're coming down. Please come soon, soon, soon. I can't wait! I just love it when you give me an oral climax!"

"Hmm-m-m," mused Princess. "What the hell? 'Oral climax'? What's that? Well, I think I know what she means, but isn't something really yummy and delicious to eat an 'oral climax'? Ooops! Here comes Randy!"

Princess quickly stuffed the letter back into the envelope and returned it to the table just as Randy reentered the room with a mug full of coffee for her. Her heart was racing as she mimed a waking stretch. "Thanks, Randy."

"Gee! I've never brought a woman to my parent's house before." he said. "You'd better leave pretty soon. No telling when they'll be back. I don't want them freaking out."

She thought Randy was a wimp, afraid of his parents and all, but he was a hell of a trumpet player. Princess had always wanted to be a groupie but was beginning to think that he wasn't the one she wanted to follow around.

She finished her coffee, got ready for the day, and said her good-byes. She expected to see him around but somehow the lust was gone. They'd had a night of eating her good food, which she cooked to perfection in his parent's kitchen and the sex was pretty good. He was cute and he was nice but she couldn't see herself hooking up permanently with a concrete contractor, which was his day job. Plus her real love was Timmy.

The drive from Downeast along the coast was magical; bright with autumn sunshine glowing off leaves of every color. The sun hit the sea, creating sparkles like silver tinsel. The breeze was heady with a hint of chill. Princess was glad she had worn her knitted cape. The scenery and the vividness of the autumn colors, backlit by the afternoon sun, were so intense she had to pull her '75 VW over when she came to a rest area. She sat in the car and tears rolled down her cheeks. "There can be nothing more beautiful than this," she hiccuped. "This could almost make me a believer."

Soon, thoughts of the "oral climax" returned and she smiled, then laughed out loud, wiped the tears from her cheeks and started up the VW.

Miles later, Princess pulled into her usual spot in the woods and saw that Gargoyle's ancient, rusted truck was there. Gargoyle was a good friend but sometimes his behavior was abrasive and irritating. Princess was both glad to see he was at her Tree House, and angry because his truck was such a wreck and she didn't want anyone to see it parked there. She wondered if Gargoyle had picked up Lorenza on his way over. The thought of seeing Lore made her feel happy and lifted her heart.

She jogged up the path to the house through the locust and maple woods and the long vibrant rays of the late afternoon sun. She smelled the sweetness of wood burning in the stove.

Although hers was a real tree house it wasn't up in the tops of the trees. Four stout locust trees stood as corner posts. They were still rooted in the ground and cut off at eleven feet holding the steep roof. The building was a fourteen by fourteen foot square and twenty-five feet tall with cedar shingles on the outside. She jumped up on the rock stoop and pushed the door open. There sat horsey-looking Gar smoking a Camel, his mane of graying hair combed back neatly, waving down his back. He was watching the flames licking the mica window of the woodstove. No Lore.

Disappointed and starting to feel irritated, she said, "Whose butts are you smoking? Those mine? Why don't you get your own?!"

"Hey, slow down. I got you a bottle of Jack. C'mon. Have a drink with me!"

"I'd rather eat broken glass," Princess mumbled, bristling.

"What's that?" said Gar.

"Oh, uh, I said, 'sure pour me a glass.'"

Gargoyle unfurled his lanky frame and poured the drink.

"Thanks," she said. Relaxing into the warmth of the whiskey and feeling a little more kindly toward Gar, she began to tell him about the night with Randy and the pink letter. "I used up almost half of the food stamps buying a slab of swordfish. I cooked it with capers in a white wine reduction. It was really delicious, if I say so myself, but I think it was wasted on him!"

Gar laughed, "Lucky guy! You should have tried it out on me! So, what about the letter?"

Princess told him about the pink passion and laughed. "I think we should start a Friday night club and call it the Oral Climax Social Club. What do you think? We'll invite everyone over to eat yummy stuff and dance."

"Sounds good to me!"

Another drink or two later Princess put on a Talking Heads tape and the two friends practiced dance routines 'til the sun disappeared behind the distant ocean. She said, "Let's go get Lore and see what she thinks of the club idea. Bring the bottle."

They left in the rusty old truck which ran rough on gas fumes and bald tires.

Princess had been laid off from work for the winter and was living on Workman's Comp and food stamps. Lorenza worked occasionally, doing some house painting. Gar didn't work at all, although he considered getting up in the morning, eating breakfast, tidying up, making phone calls and reading, "work." He was living on credit from the local grocery store while he waited for an insurance claim check, and was able to supply himself, and the girls with gasoline and gourmet food items. Bets had been laid about town as to whether Gar would ever see a cent of money from the claim, but meanwhile the grocer, convinced by Gar's smooth-talk, had faith that he'd get his due. Gargoyle said he was writing a play but so far the girls hadn't seen any evidence of it.

When Princess and Gar arrived at Lorenza's, the girls screamed and jumped up and down with excitement and hugged, as they always did. "Hi, sweetie! How's my crazy, insane friend?" Lore gushed.

"Hello Lore! I see you're just as nuts as always. We saved you some of the booze." Lore's eyes were dark and wild, her grin wide, with beautiful white teeth. Her long, brown hair flowed around her shoulders and down her back. Between Lorenza's 6'2", and Gar's 6'5", Princess felt like a shrimp when they were all together.

Gar brought forth the bottle, now half empty. "What's happening?" he said.

"Still having plumbing problems," said Lore. "No plumbing, that's the problem!" She laughed. "The water heater is under water. I think it should be the other way around, don't you? Shouldn't the water be in it instead?" She couldn't stop giggling. "Hey Gar, why don't you go down cellar and fix it?"

"Ha ha. Have some Jack," he said. "I've been down there. Once is enough!"

The idea of Gar fixing anything, besides a drink, made the girls laugh even more.

Lorenza's cellar was a wet, dark cave of fallen-in rocks and granite blocks, with a littered mud floor. The stairs were half rotten and most of them had joined the debris on the dank floor. The single, naked light bulb hung from a frayed black wire that had been installed in 1929 by her granddad. The ragged insulation which clung to the wire had become fodder for porcupines, but even the critters had moved on years ago. Lore repeatedly replaced the bulb but the light continued to short out.

"Saint said he'd come take a look if I give him a kiss," she said.

"He'll do anything for a kiss," said Princess. "By the way, he should be the first one we invite to the Club on Friday."

"What club?" Lore asked.

"Go ahead and tell her," said Gar.

"Jeeez, you won't believe this, Lore. I spent last night with that trumpet player, Randy..."

"Oh, yeah, I guess you couldn't wait for Timmy!"

"No, no, no... that's not what I was going to tell you. Listen, I sneaked a look at this perfumed letter next to the bed and..." Princess told her the whole story. "I decided we should start a club called O.C.S.C. The Oral Climax Social Club. What do you think? We'll invite everyone over and have delicious food to eat!"

"Didn't I say you're nuts, already? This proves it, you crazy girl. But... I think it's an excellent idea!"

"Let's go back to the Tree House," Princess said. "We can make some supper and plan for a party on Friday. Hey, Gar, put a couple big logs in the stove, and let's go! Lore can call Saint from my place. It's not a toll call."

She was getting cold and uncomfortable in Lore's damp house. There was no heat except for a small fire in the woodstove in the living room. Lore was afraid to make a roaring fire in it, even though she'd just bought the stove and had a new chimney built.

The three pals left Lorenza's, taking what remained of the Jack Daniels. They climbed into the truck, and returned to the Tree House. It was warm and cozy inside. They drank 'til the bottle was empty while making a list of people to invite and the food they would eat at the first meeting of the O.C.S.C.

All day Friday, Princess cleared the small house arranging the chairs and seats around the perimeter of the main room. She put new candles in holders, selected some good dancing tapes and fired up the wood cook stove to make a boeuf bourguignon with lots of red wine and fresh egg noodles. She would pair it with a salad of freshly picked spinach from the local farm stand. She was peeling apples for her special pie when Gar arrived with Lore. He brought triple creme champignon, a double creme bleu, and Stilton cheeses, some fancy imported crackers from the grocery and another bottle of Jack. Lorenza brought Breyer's vanilla ice cream to go with the pie and the custard-filled eclairs which Princess had made the day before: their chocolate ganache icing was being kept warm on the back of the stove 'til dessert time. A wedge of rat cheddar to accompany the pie was the last item Gar pulled from the grocery bag.

Lorenza and Gargoyle sat around smoking and drinking and arranging the cheese platter, while Princess fussed with the finishing touches to the meal.

Saint, carrying a six-pack of light beer, was the first guest to arrive. He was met with happy exclamations and lots of hugs. Saint was well named. He was a big guy with a great warm heart, handsome, with thick, dark, curly hair and a bushy, black beard. He was quite a bit older than the three friends. Saint would do anything and fix anything for free — or a kiss — plus he loved to party. He loved the girls. They laughed and always had a good time together. Lore dragged him to a corner where she could tease him and discuss the problems she was having in her cellar. He must have agreed to help her out. It looked as though he got more than one kiss.

Soon the Tree House was filled with partygoers: Mick and Sue, Butch from the inn down the road, and Deedee. Mick, already drunk, shuffled to a chair in another corner and immediately passed out. Each time there was a knock on the door, Princess's nerves jumped with anticipation at seeing Timmy, who was supposed to be coming with his roommate, Doc. Timmy was her new love, but theirs had to be a vicarious affair. Timmy's fiancee, Barbie, had told him if he fooled around on her again, their relationship was over and the marriage was off. Of course Princess did her best to seduce him, she wanted him so badly. "What rotten luck!" she thought. "This is the one I really, really want and I'm not supposed to touch! Ow!"

She thought of the romantic night they had met; an evening wedding during a huge wind and rain storm a month before. When his intense blue eyes met her wild green ones, they were both hooked. They drank lots of champagne. Their dancing had been slow and sexy, then wild like the stormy night. The sleeve had accidentally been torn from his thrift store shirt and then her dress, not so accidentally, from her shoulder. The erotic dream ended when all the guys left the party to secure their boats. Gar returned to take Princess home but Timmy never came back. Who was he? Where was he? She was frantic! Gar knew his name and not much more; just enough to find his number. Gar heard he was building a 34' wooden sloop with help from a local boat builder.

When Timmy finally arrived at the Tree House with Doc, Princess and Timmy ran into each others arms and hugged, spinning around and around in circles. They both smiled 'til Princess thought their faces would split open. Her heart melted and brimmed with happiness.

Doc was supposed to divert Princess's attention from Timmy so he would remain faithful to Barbie. Princess thought Doc was cute and he thought the same of her, but there were no sparks flying. Doc sat and talked with Sue while she sewed doll clothes to sell, and drank whiskey with him.

139

After Lore convinced Saint to help her out with her plumbing problem, she gave Butch a well-deserved foot massage. His poor feet were overworked, split, cracked, and sore from standing on them everyday at the inn. Butch was quickly lulled to insensibility. Gar sought out Deedee, tall and curly-haired. They'd been friends for years, but Deedee didn't feel a bit romantic about him even though Gar was constantly trying to get her into bed. Princess and Deedee often laughed about Gar's bad luck with women. He was frustrated and didn't understand that it was his irritating attitude which totally worked against him. He thought he was God's gift to women but his flirting was embarrassing. The girls often wondered why some guys could get away with that behavior, while others, like Gar, couldn't.

The Tree House was warm and festive. The guests were happy, devouring the cheeses and crackers and drinking Jack Daniels. Princess reluctantly let go of Timmy and announced, "Time for an Oral Climax!"

Princess brought out the exotic bourguignon and the guests served themselves. The beef was tender and deliciously seasoned. It was rich but not heavy, perfectly paired with the fresh, delicate, handmade egg noodles, a perfect union of textures and flavors. For the salad, she tossed the crisp, fresh spinach with her lemon and olive oil dressing, added toasted pine nuts, hard-boiled eggs and crispy bacon from her neighbor's small farm. She sprinkled a dash of umeboshi vinegar and then grated Grana Padano and minced, fresh garlic over it all. From then on until the serving dishes were emptied, there were murmurs of "Mmmm!" and "Ohhh-h-h!" and "Yummm!" and "Ah-h-h-h!" as the guests patted their full bellies.

The October moon rose, slid past the locust trees and dappled the maple leaves against the windows. The candlelight was soft.

Dessert was served; the custard-filled eclairs were delicate and light yet rich, with the chocolate ganache. Then came the apple pie, not too tart, not too sweet, savory with spices, and baked to perfection served with the rat cheese and creamy ice cream on the side. Everyone was totally blissed out. Lore was the first to exclaim, "I've just had multiple oral climaxes!" All the guests agreed. "I've had three!" "I had five!!" "Fifteen for me!"

Princess turned up the volume and on went the Talking Heads. She and Gar did their new dance routines. The guests clapped and cheered, then they all took to the floor. Timmy reached for Princess. As she melted into him, a thousand butterflies fluttered around her heart. With their arms around each other, they danced wildly, then slowly, moving together, just as they had the first time, his bright blue eyes fused with her green ones. She whispered, brushing her warm lips against his ear, her soft breath making him shiver, "Please, please, Timmy. Barbie won't know! Just don't tell her!"

O.C.S.C.

"You know I want to... if it was just Barbie... but it's the whole family. They arranged it years ago!" He told her that the stress had made his back break out in boils. They both wished that this was the first time he'd cheated on Barbie, because Princess knew he had gotten away with it once, but if there was a next time, it would be all over with Barbie and her family. The other guests danced around them. "When the boat is done, let's sail to Belize," he breathed into her silky hair, continuing the fantasy.

Timmy lowered his mouth to her breast and in an instant he jerked his head up having snapped the Izod alligator off her red turtleneck with his teeth. Shocked with surprise, she screamed, then howled with laughter. The other guests joined in the hilarity as he spit the alligator into his hand and put it in his pocket to save forever.

With the romantic spell broken, Princess, Lore and Gar decided the next entertainment would be a moonlit walk with the group through the woods to the beach. Holding hands in a long line, they stumbled over roots and rocks and across the road to the trail which led to the shore.

Mick regained consciousness briefly in the empty Tree House. "What the hell...?" he said aloud to himself. "Am I dreaming? Where the f - - - is every-body? I thought I was at a party?" Then he passed out again.

The group returned, refreshed by the cool autumn night's exercise of sea-weed fights and skipping stones across watery moonbeams. They had played beach tag, had double-decker-piggy-back fights among the rocks, and moon bathed on the coarse sand of the beach.

Back up the hill, Saint was the last of the group to climb the rock stoop into the Tree House. Once inside he guffawed at the sight of Mick. "I can't believe that guy is still out. I'll never forget this!"

The guests agreed that the first meeting of the O.C.S.C. had been a tremendous success and they all looked forward to the next Friday and more oral climaxes. Princess tried to get Timmy to spend the night. He wanted to. He just couldn't and Doc made sure he didn't.

Princess and Timmy hugged long and tight promising each other to continue their romantic fantasy, and until then, whenever Princess thought of him (which was often), her heart raced and her mouth salivated, as she headed for the kitchen. ∎

Jacqueline Michaud

At the Elephant Camp

The driver led him to us, massive chains dragging,
as barefoot children stood in the yard, wary,
unsmiling – though we waved "Hello"–
mindful of their father, who eyed them also.

We climbed the scaffold, stepped off its top plank
into a large basket strapped to the elephant's back,
and set out, undulant, into the lavish surround,
keeping to a trail of pale yellow dust.

Overhead monkeys shrieked and mynas clacked
as palm fronds did a drum-brush on the breeze,
wafting the driver's warm whisky breath back to us.
When the beast slowed to a halt, dropped its dump,

a rider up front cracked to colleagues in back,
"We'll want a full report, men." Everyone laughed then,
but the driver, who whacked at jumbo's trunk, jabbed it
with a long metal prod, and again we set off. Slowly

it began to dawn – that wrinkled old behemoth
must be sick of going round the same worn path
to the delight of tourists for peanuts.
Re-entering the camp, we saw a small-boned woman

in a frayed sari, baby on her hip. Nor did she wave back.
We had our photo snapped, the guide brought his jeep,
and away we drove, the view of our big adventure
growing smaller and smaller.

The Understory

From our blind we listen, hushed by dusk, for the sounds
of lapping at water's edge, massive paws, claws retracted,
matting down the weed-whacked grasses along a well kept
jungle trail. Our jeep bumps through ruts from view to view,
crossed by peacocks, blue tails trailing in languid flight.
Bison, langur, barking deer in plenty, but no tigers here
as our well-groomed guide, Sanjay, had promised.

Night falls – a chill shot through the understory. I press close
to my man as our safari winds down the tire-gouged trail.
Next morning we ride a docile elephant at the camp of a tribe
displaced when the state flooded their land for this preserve:
Nagarhole: "Snake Stream." Later, drifting in our coracle,
we follow sloth bear, plump boar ambling along the shore,
spy immobile egrets, zoom in on circling birds of prey.

"Eagle!" Sanjay points. "Vulture," one of our party whispers.
In the evening, before strolling down a petal-strewn path
to dine in the former Viceroy's hunting lodge, snug bungalow,
we watch – management politely insists – a warped nature video
in which a lethargic tiger gnaws the flesh off fly-caked prey,
as a deep British voice intones: "What's really at stake for India
is its very identity as home of the elephant and tiger."

Jacqueline Michaud

3:00 AM in Delhi

There's more to India than bad water, sir!
I didn't have the guts to say
to that rancher in the Admiral's Lounge
droning on about beggars, pollution,
hawkers of carved elephants.

These "Hindoos" aren't here for you to refuse
to haggle for, dismiss their Ganesha, ma'am!
I didn't say to his wife, who even groused
about the exchange rate. I wanted to talk about
Gomateshwara of Sravanabelagola –

words I liked the feel of leaving my mouth,
a little circus tumbling out. At the sacred gate,
we had to remove our New Balance
shoes before climbing the many steps more than 600
our guide claimed led to a naked Jain saint,

that monolithic statue carved from a mountain
in the first millennium so we, in the second,
could pose between its colossal toes. (Looking up,
my face came out red.) *Fodor's* said little about that
temple, so for enlightenment, back home I went

online to learn Jainism arose in protest
against the sacrificial cults and extreme rituals
of Hinduism. Jains rejected the *Veda* – the oldest
scriptures of Hinduism – Vedic theories
of cosmology and a single underlying reality

as found in the *Upanishads* – sacred Hindu texts
that centuries later lit the imagination
of Schrödinger, the great theoretical physicist!
If they knew all that they rebuffed
had informed quantum mechanics,

would they have been as dismissive?
I wanted to go back, talk about that,
decry their intolerance. If I could,
would I have admitted my own cool refusal
to meet the eye of that other Jain, the double

amputee propped on a wobbly wooden dolly
racing toward us, propelled by his fists,
or the Jain girl clutching a carved saint, gesturing
beneath our tour bus window for 10, merely,
of the 1000s of rupees in my new waist wallet?

Stephen Rifkin

Signs We Speak in Those

his error stupidity live a wholly human life
you must live

the path on the bank a girl
her brown short hair his age halved

a thorn
of barely hidden love

words pricked
and piqued and took

they were his tongue

and books whose fiction their clash of insufficient truths
they labored who shared hard ones

eyes that were the grayish sky of morning in a second took the sky
took it from him their ample reader now a ruminator

of the river light through trees where it presaged something deep he joked
a weather man his new ancillary career for helpfulness

like
selling ice cream at the apocalypse hers

the sensitive silence stood and the river's riven light
among leaves filled with lost meanings

because there is no perfect river there is only water
and water's film and light

the tongue seeks in a fool's boundary he saw

not science or silence
or hidden music not her

eyes closed set upon the river's deeper course

he rose on words those then reticence
that lives long in the mind still

and lies
among the irrevocable said

Phil Schirmer

Notes From A Lovesick Dragon

I have been on my belly for over a month now, waking
occasionally when the damp floor makes my ribs ache.

My head isn't right.

There is green slime on my scales and my computer keeps
crashing. I stopped reading emails anyway – just a bunch of
villagers whining about me raiding their towns or some
company from New Jersey trying to sell me vinyl siding,
obviously unaware that I live in a cave.

I almost killed you.

But you looked so tiny in your white dress and those
little white boots with a hundred buttons that princesses
always seem to wear. So I sat down beside you instead
and you told me about catching fireflies on summer
evenings and eating the middle of Oreo cookies first and
how you hate to get cat food on your fingers. And I told
you things about me too, like, for instance, that I have to
travel much further now to find new villages to raid. But
when I looked into your eyes I realized that the walls
we were tearing down were holding up a very heavy roof.

So I left you there in that ruined town and flew home.

But I was still hungry so I scorched the senior center on
my way out and dined on a couple of tough old ladies,
only to find that one of them was your Aunt Gwendolyn
who used to cook up a three-bean chili that would make
a beached whale dance like a Chihuahua in a frying pan.

I'm sorry I ate her.

George

George is hiding under a chair in shadows
the color of his fur.
I dangle a string.
He watches.

Swinging the string back and forth doesn't work.
George apparently sees no advantage in chasing things
that swing back and forth. I lay the string on the carpet
and give it a slight jerk – a wounded animal limping away.
The end of his tail twitches.

George spends his days apart from the other two cats,
noticing things through windows. He is studious.
He doesn't play. A nuclear physicist, no doubt,
in a previous life, patiently enduring jokes
about his bow tie and white socks.

I tug the string. George bats at it tentatively. I tug it again.
In a motion of almost incomprehensible speed
he breaks from the shadows and pins the string to the rug.
A growl rolls out from the cave of his chest.

George,
who sneaks to the pantry twice a day for food and water,
is now chasing Winky down the stairs,
and up the stairs.
He makes a circuit around the room and stops
spread-eagled in the center of the rug.
His eyes are embers, his fur a charred shell.

In a mad, wild dash he leaps onto the table and slides
head-on into a lamp that falls to the floor and shatters
with a sound probably louder than any he has ever created.
Before the lampshade stops rolling, George is back
under the chair, merging with the shadows.

Soon he will retire to his windowsill, compose himself
as carefully as any rumpled-suited physicist would who
has just witnessed the awesome power he is capable
of unleashing, and, without a hint of irony,
study the sun cooling to the horizon.

Stone Work

The stones arrived in early September –
twenty-six of them, the size of small refrigerators.
The truck driver hauled his belly down from the
cab and crossed the yard to speak to a woman
who was only slightly taller than his armpits.
Straight across the back, he said, is where I'd put them.
The woman smiled.
Let's put the first one here...

All afternoon the bucket-loader nudged the stones
to where the woman pointed.
Six inches back, please... A little to the right.
At five-o'clock the driver dumped a load of dirt
to fill in behind and raked it out smooth.
It's your yard, Ma'am, he said and
backed out of the driveway.

Eight months later a line of daffodils
followed the wandering contour of the wall.
Stay there, the flowers nodded
to the stones at their feet,
and they did.

To Paint a Crow

Start with a long, thin canvas, tinted gray. Paint two
yellow lines down the middle, or white dashes if you
prefer. Take it outside on a clear night and unroll it
across your lawn, your neighbor's lawn, and beyond.

Keep going. Eventually your canvas will roll out into
the morning sun, somewhere in western China.
See the peasant farmer push his hat back to squint
at the luminous highway crossing his rice paddy.

Now go back to the beginning of the canvas and cut
a hole out the shape of a crow, hunched over, eating.
Don't forget to put a slight hook at the tip of his beak.
Hold your canvas up to the night sky.

See how black your crow is now! How the darkness
swells and clenches inside him until the light itself is
broken into mean little pieces and sprinkled on the sky
like salt on a wound. Feel the strange pull of its gravity.

Finally, if you decide the painting needs a little color to
give it life, apply some deep alizarin crimson in bold
slashes under the crow's hooked beak, thinned out
just enough so that it runs and drips off the edge.

Norma Voorhees Sheard

Control

Local Headline –
"Summer people complain about deer
eating gardens and ornamental shrubs"

Shrill barking pierces the darkness –
the coyote of Sunset Crossroad.
Not the romantic
back-and-forth calls
across lonely prairie land
I had imagined.

Surely the game wardens knew
when they let them loose
on this Downeast island
ten pairs would do more
than control the whitetails;
that rabbits, fox, racoons
and pets would not be exempt
from carnage, even in daylight.

Suzette's white kitten
lifeless and bloody
near the porch steps
when the children wake.
Sandra's big cat, Tom,
ripped apart.

Kathy Gross saved her Yorkie,
screaming as she chased a pack
through her woods with a broom
before the dog was relinquished –
eleven stitches to sew its neck.

That cocky varmint
has nothing to fear
from predators here,
only brooms and sticks
or the crack of guns
in the hands of fed-up locals.

Norma Voorhees Sheard

Epilogue: Advent

The day before this first Sunday
I unwrap blue tissue –
the angel you gave me last year
when, together, we set up wisemen
and shepherds, Mary and Joseph,
the little baby asleep
on painted hay.

You had cast the plaster angels
from molds you made at St. Barnabas,
you told me, handling them fondly
one by one, apologizing for
the rough edges of their wings.
Too weak from radiation
and chemo to care about holidays,

you wanted only the worn creche.
While you dozed, I arranged the angels
on a window sill above the scene
and noticed how their heads tilted
slightly to one side as though
contemplating what was below:
the stable, the brown donkey,
the labored breath of the woman,
her arms curled around her knees.

from: The Bondstone poems

Predator

for David (Fudd) McDonald

As top of the local food chain,
the coyote treads brazen
but careful at cove head,
avoiding sink holes
in the mud flats.
His long legs
don't want to hold back;
he wants to prance
under the warming sun.
Flicking his scrawny tail
he heads for high ground
near the wood line,
not far from cottages
vacant all winter.
He has already done in
Fudd's cat, Mr. Bean,
who sat every morning
on a marsh log, waiting
for voles and mice,
whiskers twitching impatiently
as the tide edged closer.

Norma Voorhees Sheard

Gloria
For John Bicknell

You would have admired the poetry
of moonlight shining on water,
the clouds backlit, steered
by a brisk January wind
that sends your spirit soaring
beyond our horizon.
Every season was your joy,
every challenge a new day.
But just now we will miss
that sporty wool cap pulled low,
your thick mittens, the scarf
wrapped around your throat.
We thought you would go on forever,
the way the moon always shines
on the bay, the way your voice
will sing the first glorious star
into the evening sky.

Previously Published: Off the Coast

August

Crickets celebrate,
rev up their engines,
chirp their glee.

Cicadas practice
their long one-note arias.

Fan full throttle
scarcely stirs the indolent air.
Heat oozes around the edges,
marinates muscle,
softens bone,
turns man and beast to fillet.

Julian A. Waller

Celebration

The gulls have gathered
from the far reaches of the bay.
They have booked the red barn by the shore
and are deep in festivities,
loud in gullian conversation.

The young ones wheel
around the schooners, line up
for food at the greenshackled fishing boat,
drop meals and pass-throughs
in inconvenient places.

The old ones sit rocking on the rooftop,
survey the scene, reminisce
about the heyday
of the old sardine factory,
when portions were much bigger
and takeout could be gotten
all three shifts, seven days a week.

Julian A. Waller

Laundry Library

I endure another day at the island laundry,
dingy edifice for clean living,
two rows of machines, here and there
posted "Out of Order,"
two chairs for the week-worn,
ten open maws
ready to accept damp offerings
for the final bake to dryness
before customers stagger out,
lugging their resurrected lives
neatly folded in baskets, boxes, bags.

I examine the back counter, a mausoleum
of outdated newspapers and magazines
that promises little but disappointment.
Nonetheless, everyone tries it.

Two copies of *The Ladies Home Journal*
top the heap, dog-eared, one
with pages pasted together
by a sugar-laden drink
available in the vending machine.
I set them aside.

The *Bangor Daily News*, three days old,
reports bombings in Iraq, insults from Iran,
fires, injuries and other local mayhem,
and national financial mischief.
But I am war-and-wreck-weary.
This too is cast aside, perhaps useful
for someone to mop up spilled detergent.

A glitzy real estate brochure,
pictures on every lacquered page,
promises untold comfort and relaxation
if only I can overlook my poverty
and the exorbitant asking price.

A fresh layer looms, a dozen copies,
totally pristine, of *The Watchtower*,
the Sermon on the Mount miraculously
transported to this humble Laundromat.
Each copy invites me to accept Jesus
and repent the awful gravity of my sins.
I pull back quickly, certain
that my time spent here is penance enough.

At last I spy a copy of *The New Yorker*,
well worn, welcomed and welcoming.
I grab a seat, open a page, and wrap myself
in the fuzzy warmth of an Ed Koren cartoon.

Julian A. Waller

Morning Matters

Bolt upright in bed – obligatory posture
for thirty minutes after taking my osteoporosis pill –
I sit reading Billy Collins' *Sailing Around The Room*.
I follow this morning regimen
hoping to avoid a gradual transformation
to absolute spinelessness.

Outside a wind wails ceaselessly,
cranks up its tune, insinuates itself
past the half-opened storm window,
ululates between window and screen,
a wordless song, infinitely sad,
as the sound runs up and down
a scale of its own making.

Seagulls screech their messages over the water,
talk to themselves, to each other,
to lobstermen at sea and on shore,
to whoever will listen, even to me.

Now they perch on the rooftop,
hoping I have skipped a dose,
hoping I too will sail around the room,
hoping the wind will carry me out,
hoping they will have
a good, easy, spineless meal,
not some hard-shelled mollusk
they must drop repeatedly to open,
but a soft-skinned substantial meal,
a meal they can pick at.

Julian A. Waller

Reading

She reads to the blind man.
He watches.
Every word, carefully spoken,
pushes past ears barely adequate.
She pauses.
What are you thinking?

When you were young,
just beginning school,
you used to read to Mom and me.
I can see you now. I can see her...

Please, continue.

Like Hattifatteners

They're like Hattifatteners,
She said. I knew what she meant,
Having read Jansson, though in translation.
She said, The way they mill about,
All tall, with their big eyes.
Those staring big eyes.

We sat on a crusty boulder,
Crumbling blue lichen under our pink heels,
Our toes stretched out over the giddy green sea.

I raised my chin to nod. A cormorant
Swept by, searching the swells that
Shrugged their way toward an island.
Out of the eastern horizon, like a peacock,
A schooner arose, over-masted, it seemed
From our talus-bound viewpoint,
Skerry, really.

And pale, she said. Tall and pale,
And the way they drift around in groups like that.
Bunches of swaying Hattifatteners. She sighed,
And leaned back on her elbows.

I leaned over my knees, and in the blur,
Where blue met green, saw St. James' Park,
A tall, tailored back, suave as the black swan.

Can you stand it?
She was saying.
What?
That finger waggling.
Why do they do that? Fluttering fingers,
And mumbling. Only they know
What they are saying. She flopped back and
Dropped onto her face a handkerchief,
Quite frayed.

Wings akimbo, the cormorant stood
Bedraggled by useless plunges.
Beyond, the island waited for the schooner,
Its scalp of firs prickling.

The lichen, with symbiotic stubbornness,
Clung to their granite cushion.
I rubbed at their impression on my thigh, tracing
In the maze, the way to the stone footbridge,
Turn of shoulder, gaze of grey
An embrace light as a mist net.

Suddenly there they are. Close-ranked,
Mumbling, or silent, I don't know
Which is worse. Your hair stands on end,
Not surprising. -- Yes, I remember. --
It's their electricity. They show up
Looking for thunderstorms, and leave
In a flotilla of messages set adrift. Sailing
Away in those little round boats.

For a while, she read, I began a letter.
The whisperings of pages and pen point
Were soon only those of pages.
On the parapet, a hand opens,
Down long fingers roll the last of the petits fours,
Cake crumbs tumbling to the hopeful ducks.

I wonder what it's like in a coracle,
I said, That's how they come.
Who?
Hattifatteners, I said.

Red Right Return

Ava kicked free of the tangled sheets and sat up. Out the window this April morning sea and sky lay pale and impassive. Boulders held the harbor on two sides, each sprawling, tawny back streaked with run-off from a spiky mane of spruce. Blue and green lay in between. Yet there was no horizon; not, anyway, the thin seam where ocean meets welkin, the fissure through which a vessel, bold enough, might slip away. A dark shape stood in the space where such an horizon ought to have been, a distant land mass that appeared as a door slammed shut on the harbor. Indeed, the sailboats never seemed to go anywhere, but idled like toys in a forgotten pool. Beyond the boats, amid a scattering of islets and skerries, a red nun buoy rocked side to side, an agitated sentinel. Ever in the wind and waves seemed an odd place for a nun. Mariners were meant to steer close, but not too close, keeping her to port or starboard, whichever it might be.

Ava buttoned into cotton blouse, shorts, topped both with a wool pullover, the kind those intrepid Norse fishermen wear, and turned her back on the unreliable scene.

The view, while solid-looking enough to be frustrating, was, at the same time, annoyingly changeable. Emerald and sapphire. Steel and silver. There were days when the ocean and the atmosphere swapped sides, green above, blue beneath. Often it all melded, one vast white-grey billow that smothered harbor, village, house. She crossed the cold, creaking boards to put the kettle on.

Wrecking cobwebs and clearing drawers of spider skeletons had occupied the hours of her first autumn there. Flotsam of decades, covering almost every horizontal surface, she left undisturbed. Each sea shell had been, at one time, to someone, a treasure, held high and sparkling on a sandy, outstretched hand, kept in a pocket, given a reassuring turn every now and then; later shaken out of the laundry and placed in the front of the pile of urchins, sea glass, sand dollars. Some bore names and dates: *Seal Cove, 1986* inside a small red carapace; *D & M, 1952* on a smooth blue and white stone.

In contrast to the house, which was sparsely furnished, the shed was packed with chairs, lamps, motors, fuel cans, boxes of junk, and, behind a mildewed mattress, a twelve-foot skiff. From beneath its plastic tarp of retirement came the idea of exploring by boat. Each time she ventured out, a different island presented yet another unique shoreline from which to collect marine plants. Every cove offered expectations of, or at least hope for, an eye-to-eye with a harbor seal, or a breathy glimpse of dolphin. Each skerry extended a flat-enough rock upon which to sketch, a patch of sand for a picnic lunch, and, sometimes, a tiny cove for bathing – though this chill expanse of the North Atlantic, skirted by warmer currents, each year took fewer and fewer minutes to turn feet red.

She usually returned before sunset, gliding past the stilt-legs of the Harbor Café to the dock. But the times dusk found her still far from shore, such as when the motor refused to start and she had to row, when the terns had disappeared, and the hills were black silhouettes that echoed and mocked the thumping oars, she took heart and was guided by the tiny yellow eyes of the café. After each r–eturn, she bailed with a cut-away milk jug.

One afternoon, she looked up from bailing to meet the gaze of a face in the café window. A hand reached up beside the face and waved. Subsequent afternoons, she'd motor up, and there he'd be, sitting on the dock. He wore brown corduroy trousers, a tweed jacket, leather boat shoes, and a grey, woolen driving cap. He looked to be around eighty years-old.

"Ahoy!" he called out, from three feet away.

"Hi." She threw a line around a bollard.

"You're not Rita Hayworth."

She concentrated on securing the line.

"Did anyone ever tell you you look like Rita Hayworth?"

The only other being anywhere near, a herring gull atop a piling, raised his wings in a shrug.

Ava's knot repertoire was limited, unlikely to include what sailors use; but once, on a mountain trek, she had been shown the bowline. The rabbit comes out of the hole, goes around the tree …

His eyes were on her; the scrutiny of which confused the rabbit, and the tree.

… the rabbit goes back into the hole …

He talked on, with a smile eager and inquisitive. The gull squawked, drowning out his words, except for "It Girl." The old man's presumptive discourse was at once off-putting, perplexing, and amusing. If he were looking for glamour, he was certainly in the wrong place. Women and men alike, in this corner of the world, wore drab shirts and trousers, year round. Glamour was as likely to be found here as was a quetzal.

She dropped the line – the uniquely combined sheepshank/granny knot that had materialized looked like it would hold – and strode up the dock.

One cool June morning, on the walk back from the post office, the breeze swept her gaze to where he stood on the dock looking out across the water. He saw her and called out "Halloo!"

"Look there," he said, when she had joined him. "That's my boat." He pointed to a craft farthest out. White above, red along the water line, the sail-boat tugged at its mooring. "Someone else owns her now. But they don't take much interest. She needs bailing. See how low she rides?"

How high or low a boat should ride was a mystery, but she nodded. His son had sold the boat, declaring it was too much for his father to handle, and he didn't have time to help him; he'd installed him in an assisted-living apartment in a retirement complex a mile from the village. And the son, with wife and children, found a house in another town.

They walked back up the wooden planks to the beat of an old swing tune from the café.

"Will you let me buy you a cup of coffee?" he said.

"Tea," she said, as they slid into a booth, "with milk."

His name was Richard Hanson. Summers of his youth had been spent sailing. He'd sailed everywhere and anywhere between Martha's Vineyard and Bar Harbor. During his service in the Navy he had been stationed in Brazil and Newfoundland. He'd married a woman who had had the best of intellect and good looks. He'd taught at Bates College for thirty years; there was a chair named in his honor. With a quiet smile he leaned toward her and said:

"I'm a genius."

A gale, raging for two days, afforded hours in which to read, listen to music, and arrange sprigs of rockweed and wrack into journals, until the power went out. Booming thunder shook the windows. Lightning lit the harbor. In that moment, the farthest boat gleamed like a streak of lipstick in the dark. A seaweed candle lit the way to a tall blue taper, which poured light onto the gowns in her steamer trunk. She slipped into the red silk and, when the music resumed, waltzed in the glow of wavering flames.

Torrents of rain had fallen, yet she found the boat nearly dry. A note taped to the throttle stick said: "Do you like fish chowder?" A potted azalea appeared on her front porch. The following week a strange, purple-green tropical plant with large heart-shaped leaves found itself crowded inside her screen door dangling a note: "Will you let me buy you dinner? Friday?" No, she couldn't do dinner. Not Friday. Not any day. She had her research in the evenings, through which she was well-enough sustained by tea and whatever happened to be in the biscuit tin. So they met Wednesdays, in a booth, at what became "their table," the one with the top that wobbled, for a luncheon of chowder and salad, respectively. Afterwards, he always asked for rhubarb crumble, a delicacy they never had, that never appeared.

She began to refer to him as "Old Richard" to differentiate him from two other Richards – one a teen, another middle-aged – and also as a way to head off neighbor, and café manager, Doris, greeting her with "How's it going with your boyfriend?" or "Your boyfriend was in this morning looking for you." He was more than thirty years older. But clearly he craved company. And, thinking about it, one had to admit his warmth and his wit were compelling. He had more *joie de vivre* than most younger people. He was creaky and wobbly. He dropped things. He forgot things. He wobbled, but only when he was doing things of little importance. She came to realize that when he rowed the skiff, when he played the piano, he was steady and graceful.

The outboard had just leapt into life one hot afternoon in August, when Old Richard appeared, lifting the line from the bollard.

Ideas of a day alone, collecting, thinking… , *téte â téte* with whimbrel or hermit crab, flew off like spores from a trodden puffball. His look was, for all the world, that of a street urchin before a toy shop window.

"Climb aboard," she said.

He sat in the bow, facing her with wide grin, and eyes that rivaled the sparkling waves. Wisps of white hair danced a jig on his head. She turned the throttle up. His fingers tightened on the gunwales. They buzzed ahead in a splatter of salty spray. The skiff, seemingly happy with his presence in the bow, glad of the balance, perhaps, parted the swells with ease.

"Where are we going?"

"Ben Gunn Island."

"Where?"

The island rose out of the sea, a graceful arc, like a wave, white rock on the long side, green scrub on the steep side. They dragged the skiff up the beach, and lay back in the sand.

"You brought cheese, I hope." he said.

"Of course."

Two terns wheeled around each other. He hated the retirement center, he said. It was full of old people; old people who never did anything, just sat around. One of the terns sliced into the swells like the thinnest of skipping stones. Ava kept her eyes on it as though hope boosts the chance of a prize; but the lissome hunter came up empty. Worse, Richard was saying, it was full of old people who never wanted to do anything.

They clambered over rocks bedraggled with sea lettuce and stringy green algae to the other side. She went ahead, pushing out of her mind a picture of him falling. She would not look back, but made her way through throngs of mussels, barnacles, and limpets, to a herd of pink-speckled boulders. He sank into the sand beside her, and held out the whorled shell of some seafaring gastropod, violet and white.

"A rare one." He looked out over the bay. "See those patches on the water? Those roundish places, where the surface looks different? Those are cat's paws. Sailors look for those. That's where you pick up a wind."

She handed him a slice of cheese.

"I knew a man who had once been marooned," he said, "stranded for years. What do you think he missed?"

"What?"

"Not cheese."

"What, then?"

"Romance." He ran his thumb along the curving line of the shell. "Love," he said looking up with a smile.

The air was pink and fragrant, sweetened by sea heather, wild roses, and the setting sun, in what might have been a garden nook, except there was no chorus of songbirds, just a solitary tern aloft in empyreal hesitation.

The motor went in for repairs, and when it was ready they went around by road. Old Richard offered to pilot the skiff back across the bay. She drove back and waited on the dock. After thirty minutes her mind's eye saw the skiff flipping across a hidden reef, an ancient mariner flying through the air. She forced herself to sit on a bench. How silly it was to imagine such things. She waited. The rocks waited. The tide, not waiting, dropped. More rocks waited. Finally a gnat on a seed pod appeared. The woolen-capped gnat on motoring along on the silver and blue seed pod shot to one side of the red nun buoy – very likely the wrong side. He disappeared behind an islet. After a space of two deep breaths, the gnat emerged, spun 'round, went back the way he had come, then headed toward the green can buoy and the high seas.

A speed launch roared out from the dock. A lobster boat dodged the lurching sailboats. The gnat returned as a water-boatman, bouncing over the wake and beetling 'round mooring balls. He zigzagged, finally holding steady to whatever latitude he was at. She motioned for him to come in. He waved back. Surely there was no danger. He'd grown up on the water. He cut across the bow of the lobster boat. The entourage of gulls screeched.

"Scuppered, eh?" the lobsterman called out. He threw out a line and towed Old Richard in, spray-splattered and grinning.

Curious plants and books on quantum physics appeared regularly through August. And, regularly, the boat was missing. Of course, the old sailor would survive; he would get a lift from a passing lobsterman; but the boat? She would go home to her work, trying to shake off images of the skiff mired in kelp, or, with a hole in the hull, "scuppered."

But, after all, it was only a boat. At the same time, it was this remarkable thing called a boat.

Old Richard slid into the booth, fingers outspread on the table, grinned and stared at her. She set her book aside.

"What's a nice girl like you doing in a place like this?" he said.

His hands, dappled, purple and blotchy, sliding towards hers, stopped in the middle of the table. But here, in this town, how had she come to be here? By accident, she said. She should have gone to Paris, or Vienna. Never say *should*, or *should have*, he said.

Midway through lunch a man appeared, his son, who joined them. Ava half-listened, rummaging through the jam bowl for marmalade. The son asked his father why he'd lately missed his psychiatric sessions. Old Richard turned to her. "It's genius testing," he said. "They study my IQ." Becoming suddenly subdued, he turned back to his son and reminded him that he couldn't drive because he'd failed his license renewal exam the year before. The son's eyes stayed on his food through the rest of lunch. When he did raise his head, he looked at his father as if he were a science experiment.

Friends of Old Richard sailed up from the Chesapeake Bay. As teenagers they had learned to sail on his schooner, had adventured with him up and down the Atlantic. Now, with their wives, over dinner, they talked of old voyages, of new ones, asked his advice, toasted him, and took him aboard later that week, bound for Nova Scotia. Ava cruised alongside, past Ben Gunn Island, until she could hear the warning of the bell buoy. Old Richard did a creaky hornpipe in the stern. Ava idled where the harbor met the grey turbulence of the Atlantic, then turned around, away from the shadowy land mass. She looked back once. The schooner, passing the headland, cut through the dark shape like a paper knife and was gone.

"Teach me to dance," said the note taped to the throttle stick.
"Don't you know how to dance?"
"I want you to teach me."
"You know about music; you play the piano."
"I'm a genius."
"Yes. I know."

Loneliness dogged him. But, still, he had his math, his music, and his physical sciences, theories of which he tried to explain to her, with diagrams and figures on paper napkins. She listened. But she could not understand. He talked of the love he had for his late wife, of his passion for music. That she understood.

His manner was, as always, bright and eager. The room was dim. But his countenance lit the space between them. He leaned across the table and asked about her. Yes, she had at one time been married. It hadn't worked out. He was certainly crazy, Old Richard said, to let her go. He must have been blind as well. Yes, of course, she was fond of dancing. Teach me. When? Tonight. Where? My place. No. No. She would set up a class. A dance class. And he could be in it. He could even be the dance teacher's assistant, partner. Now that was an honor he must appreciate. As they walked down the café steps, he put his arm around her shoulders. She ducked and slipped away with a jaunty "so long."

She wondered and worried. Where was he, when her boat was gone and it was getting dark? Where was this friendship going? Where did he think it was going? She told him she could not meet for lunch any more. She had work to do.

But persistent invitations did bring her, one Saturday afternoon, to his apartment. He showed her his watercolors: his boat riding high, a tropical garden; black-and-white photographs: two grinning young men in uniform, holding medals, a girl in a wide skirt with flowers in her lap. He played the piano for her: ragtime, a waltz, and a melody she remembered from childhood: *Welcome Sweet Springtime*. The way he and the piano responded to each other, with that easy grace of long intimacy, was, at once, for the beholder, a source of satisfaction and of envy.

Autumn, quick and efficiently blustery, had the elms and maples shorn by Columbus Day. Only the oak, proud in its umber tresses, sang a breezy song. Ava continued to back away. She avoided the dock and the café.

"He was in tonight," Doris said, heading up the path to her door. "He walked in and said 'Where's the Fluffy One?' That's you, obviously."

"What else did he say?"

"Well, let's see. He commented on the menu. We had our great bread pudding," Doris said with an indignant laugh. "He still wants rhubarb crumble. I told him 'Richard, give it up!' I told him 'There is no Royal Road to Rhubarb.'" She swatted at a moth near the porch light. The moth hit the floor, righted itself, and, with one wing askew, began climbing up the door frame.

"What did he say?"

"He said, 'How would you know about that?'"

Ava pushed aside a dry hollyhock stalk to open the garden gate. There was a royal road, to somewhere.

She rarely saw him those winter months, and then only a glimpse, or a momentary "Hello." But on a February evening, when ice needles blew sideways down the street, she stepped into the café to warm up, and there he was, at their table. Tea came. They embraced the white mugs to warm their hands. He looked older, somber. He'd been to the symphony, and his grandson's play. And her? Oh, you know ….

The café was quiet, low conversations and lazy country music, until someone put on a swing CD. Old Richard's gaze went to the ketchup bottle, to the bowl of jam packets, took a turn around the room, and came back to the jam. Ava stood up. She put her hand in his.

They danced. The old beaming face returned. His feet, knees, shoulders, and arms flapped, shuffled, and jigged. He danced like a white-haired grasshopper. Swing moves he faked, but with style, with raised eyebrows, and a variety of grins for emphasis. What did it matter that people were watching? The music was there. Who wouldn't, with half the chance, tangle themselves into such a dance?

Days and nights of ice turned to ice-and-mud, then to mud season. Grubby-faced crocuses huddled beside the house. The oak loosened its grip on a few leaves. Ava took her teacup out onto the porch. She buttoned the top of her Nordic sweater. Doris called out:

"Did you hear Old Richard's in the hospital? I took that tape over, the one with his piano music on it. Don't know what good it'll do. He had a stroke."

The form in the bed hardly seemed like him. The face was cocked towards the fluorescent ceiling, mouth agape. The nurse said:

"He's sleeping, sedated."

Ava stood in the middle of the floor, waiting for the right moment, for some certain impulse that would drive her closer to the metal rail of the bed, or that one which would pull her out the door, down the sterile corridor, and out for a great chestful of verdant air. The tape-player nearly succeeded in drowning out the buzz of machinery, the hiss of tubes, the sound of his rasping breath. The recording was Richard playing, a rambling medley of tunes in a shape of his own, designed and defined by whim.

She turned toward the window. The harbor was surprisingly inviting, set out and arranged in sparkling silver and blue, everything in place and ready. The sea was scored and lined, like a zen garden. The path, imprinted here and there with cat's paws, wound through bonsai islets, around the buoy, still as a red Buddha. Raking in a perplexity of deliberation, a pensive monk had been followed by a purposeful cat.

The hospital grounds were empty and quiet, except for a pair of shoes, tattered, colorless, which hung above the lawn on a telephone wire.

Richard's arm moved across the blanket toward her. She put her hand over his. "Hey," she said. "What's all this lying about, lying down on the job?"

His mouth emitted a rasping sound.

"How do you feel?"

"I didn't want you to see me this way." His voice was a hoarse whisper.

"Well, you don't look so bad, really."

"My throat is so dry." He struggled against the sedative.

The feeling of exasperation and helplessness was crushing. Richard lay snared by machines, drugs, and the system. And there was no line to throw.

"Hey," she said. "I found a place for our dance class. We'll start as soon as you're out of here. You should be out in a couple of weeks."

His fingers tightened on hers.

"I want my share of love," he said.

He shut his eyes. She turned to the window. A breath stirred the shoes which twisted and bumped in a hapless shuffle.

His son and daughter-in-law took care of everything: arranged the funeral, had his feeding tube removed, and cancelled visiting hours.

Ava set out in the skiff one last time. The engine died near the red buoy. She gave in to the pull of the out-going tide. Leaning back, she noticed a grey, plastic shopping bag wedged under the fuel tank. A map was inside, a chart, a well-crafted, finely detailed portrait of the bay, composed of multitudes of numbers, letters, and concentric topographic lines like swirls of necklaces in a jewelry box. At the top, in a shaky hand, was written: *Rules: Red Right Return. Keep green to your left when returning. Call me for navigation help. RH.*

She drifted, alone and adrift in a procession, a vernal regatta of umber leaves. She spread the chart open across her knees. An osprey's eye view of the bay, it showed a gap between the headland and the dark shape; and channels that wound through the outer islands like paths through a maze. A bell buoy marked the way outward.

She pulled the starter cord. The outboard chugged, sputtered, and was silent. She set her foot against the gunwale and yanked the motor to life. She turned the throttle up, and, green buoy to starboard, steered the boat out over bigger swells and the great wide ocean. ∎

Contributors

Judi K. Beach is author of *Wild*, a chapbook of poems, and *Names for Snow*, a children's picture book. Her first full-length book of poems, *How Far Light Must Travel* will be published in fall 2007. She is creator of *Little Boxes of Possibilities: Prompts for Writing Practice* and *The Write Deck: Images for Writing Practice*. She has taught writing workshops for twenty-three years.

Diane Berlew started writing seriously after attending a DIWG meeting. She has taught pre-school, and worked as a counselor for emotionally disturbed adolescents. She ran a B&B in Stonington where she has lived for 23 years. She particularly enjoys writing children's stories based on those told to her by her father.

Anne Larkosh Burton, memoirist and poet, moved to an old house on Burnt Cove in Stonington six years ago expecting to find solitude in which to write her memoir. Instead she encountered a vital community of writers and artists, open and welcoming, generous with their support and critique. She was published in *Eggemoggin Reach Review Volume I* and has given numerous readings at bookstores and reading events as well as on WERU Writers Forum.

Sucha Cardoza came to writing through acting, which she studied in New York, with Irene Dailey, and New Mexico, with the late Kim Stanley. Her teachers, with whom she also worked and taught, continue to inform her life as a writer. She lives on Little Deer Isle with her dogs. She was published in *Eggemoggin Reach Review Volume I*.

Sandy Cohen, experimental psychologist, explored the neuroscience of human perception. Combining his love of art and music, Sandy helped pioneer the new art form, visualization of music, which he taught at San Francisco State University and UC Berkeley. He writes short fiction and essays. Sandy lives with his wife Edee on Little Deer Isle. Sandy's new web site, *www.sandysnaps.com* presents his digital painting, photography and writing.

Jean Davison, anthropologist and international peace activist who has spent much time in Africa, holds a Ph.D. from Stanford University. Retired from teaching at American University, Jean devotes full time to international consulting and writing; is committed to improving intercultural communication and understanding. The author of several books: *The Ostrich Wakes: Struggles for Change in Highland Kenya (2006)*, *Voices From Mutira: Change in the Lives of Rural Gikuyu Women (1989; 1996)* and *Gender, Lineage and Ethnicity in Southern Africa*. Currently working on a book about an Iraqi woman. She splits her year between Harborside, ME and Austin, TX.

CONTRIBUTORS

Bettina Dudley. My writing has ranged from scientific papers to a history of The Children's School of Science, to two science books for children, to a book on herbs, and — finally — to poetry, short story and memoir. A round-about journey, but my "Self" has at last been "escaping into the open" (as E.B. White puts it).

Betty Parker Duff earned a Masters Degree in English and PhD in History from the University of Maine in Orono. Her poetry and short stories have been published in college and regional literary magazines, and she hosts a monthly radio program on WERU community radio, Writers Forum. She has written two novels, *The Down-the-River Girl* and *Tyger Tyger*, and is currently working on an as yet untitled third novel.

Maureen Farr continues to write, make art, and enjoy life. She learned to tell stories from her Scots grandmother. When she isn't traveling, she's imagining the next adventure. In a former life, she was editor of a weekly arts magazine. Graphic design helps her pay the bills; her 7-year-old granddaugher, art, and writing keep her smiling. Since she thinks she was born in the wrong decade, if she ever found a time machine, she'd jump aboard.

Hendrik D. Gideonse. Educated as a political scientist, historian, and philosopher. Employed as an academic, government and university administrator, and policy analyst. Retired ten years, he bestows his time and attention on nature, those he loves and who love him, on public service (leading sometimes to calls he drink hemlock!), and on the essential social nature of the phenomenon of mind.

Brenda Gilchrist is author, illustrator, and designer of many publications produced by Braceypoint Press, Deer Isle, including *A Collection of Leguminous Verse: Poems & Illustrations, 2006*. Prior to moving full time to Deer Isle in 1990, she spent more than thirty years in the art books publishing business in NYC. Recipient of an Honorable Mention in the 2005 Maine Writers and Publishers Alliance's Open Writing Competition, Gilchrist's work has also appeared in *Bangor Metro, Maine Times,* and *ERR, vol. 1.*

Gayle Ashburn Hadley lives and writes on Deer Isle, off the coast of Downeast Maine. She has published in a number of genres including poetry and essay and in publications including the *Eggemoggin Reach Review* and *the Working Waterfront*. Her new novel, *Eternal Vigilance*, will be out this spring. Gayle is currently working on a collection of short stories.

CONTRIBUTORS

Barbara Hattemer. Educated at Smith College and Harvard Business School, Barbara has summered on Deer Isle all her life. She authored articles in *Parents Magazine, Yankee Magazine, Guideposts, World and I*; wrote *New Light on Day-care Research* and co-authored the book, *Don't Touch That Dial: The Impact of the Media on Children and the Family*.

David Hayman, an emeritus professor of Comparative Literature at the University of Wisconsin has published books and essays on James Joyce, Samuel Beckett and lit in general; but though he has had lifelong poetic urges, his first published poems are in *Eggemoggin Reach Review Volume I*. He continues to think of his summers on Deer Isle as the best times for creative work and enjoys the audiences and frustrations he finds there.

Nancy B. Hodermarsky, of Deer Isle, itinerant teacher in Rome, Athens, New York City, Cleveland; attorney for safe crackers, broken lives, broken marriages in western Massachusetts; daughter, sister, wife, mother, grandmother, her poetry holds close her family, her life on Deer Isle, her classical education.

Delight Immonen is a musician who has written poetry since high school in Huron, Ohio. She and her husband Gerry divide their time between Burnt Cove in Stonington, Maine and Providence, Rhode Island.

Judith Albertson Ingram has been a professional visual artist for forty years and also has spent many years writing poetry and short stories. Often, she has incorporated her poetry and sections of her journals into her paintings.

E. Michaella Keener is a retired Episcopal Priest, most recently from Pennsylvania where she was the first woman rector in the Diocese. She founded a soup kitchen, The Shepherd's Kitchen, and was instrumental in developing a shelter named Shepherd's Place. She sees her experiences in the field of drug addiction as a nurse, social worker and community organizer integral to her ministry with the homeless.

David Lund, a native New Yorker, has been a devoted summer resident of Deer Isle since 1962. His work as a painter and a poet has shared similar concerns. Over time, the tones of the paintings and poetry have increasingly shared a dialogue. His paintings, known for their evocative imagery and color, are represented in national collections such as the Corcoran Gallery, the Baltimore Museum, and the Whitney Museum.

CONTRIBUTORS

Deborah Wedgwood Marshall. Desendant of the great potter, Josiah Wedgwood, schooled by Quakers, she attended the University of Florence, Italy. A lifelong writer, she has been rejected by The New Yorker. She spent all her summers in Sargentville. Returning 35 years ago, she lived in a tree house for 20 years. She now lives on Little Deer Isle. She was published in *Eggemoggin Reach Review Volume I*.

Jacqueline Michaud's work has appeared in *American Letters & Commentary, CELAAN, Florida Review, New England Review, New Laurel Review, Rock & Sling, U.S.1 Worksheets*, and the anthology, *Voices from the Robert Frost Place*, among others. Her recent work includes translations of poetry by contemporary Francophone writers, and a collection of poems by the late 20th century French poet, Jacques Prévert. Michaud, who received her BA in French Literature from Skidmore College, lives in Stonington, ME.

Stephen Rifkin keeps his breath and being attuned writing poems and sometimes short stories. He is readying a collection composed in Deer Isle and North Adams. Besides reading and writing, his occupation includes ruminative walking, visiting his wife's fabulous garden, planning returns to D.I. He was a founding member of Deer Isle Writers' Group. Earlier, he taught English.

Phil Schirmer lives in Sargentville, Maine, and paints in egg tempera, using eggs he steals from his wife's pet chickens. Before moving to Maine, he was a staff writer for an arts and entertainment weekly and art director of a magazine about horses.

Norma Voorhees Sheard is a member of two Deer Isle Writer's groups, and an away member of *US 1 Poets' Cooperative* in Princeton, NJ. During the year she also participates with the Narramissic Notebook, Salt Coast Sages and H.O.M.E. poets in Orland. Maine journals in which her work has appeared are: *Puckerbrush, Animus, Off The Coast, Sakana,* and *ERR, Vol.1*. Other work currently appears in the *Paterson Literary Review* and *US 1 Worksheets*.

After decades of doing scientific writing as a public health physician and researcher, **Julian Waller** succumbed in 1994 to the siren song of poetry. Now retired from the faculty of the University of Vermont he is active as a poet and mixed media sculptor both at his Deer Isle summer residence and his winter home in the San Francisco Bay area.

Marcy Willow, winner of the Bridport Prize for Fiction and for Poetry, among other awards, has an MA in English Literature and an MFA in Creative Writing. She writes in New York, London, and in a wind-buffeted stone cottage on the edge of a green sea. Work on her novels, stories, and poems is interrupted only by evenings of dancing, and by an annual mountaineering expedition.